Dr. Ripper's Fabricated Freaks

by Rich Nairn

To Vanessa, Welcome to my World of Weird!

For Mary,

*Talented actress, free spirit, great friend.
Always in my thoughts.*

DR RIPPER'S FABRICATED FREAKS
© 2016 by Rich Nairn

All rights reserved. The book author retains sole
copyright to his or her contributions to this book.

Introduction by
Mr. R. Nairn

Back in 2001, while working as a projectionist in a cinema I created mini comics inspired by the weirdness around me.
These comics were titled,
"Dr. Ripper's Multiplex".
The story was based on a lunatic asylum that got it's funding by doubling as a multiplex cinema, and it gave me an excuse to vent about the frustrations of working in that environment. It wasn't until the second comic that I created Dr. Ripper himself as an immortal doctor who was in charge of that demented establishment.
Seven years later I was working as a caricaturist at a strange little Victorian theme park in Kent, England, and once more inspired by my bizarre surroundings, Dr. Ripper came back into my life.
This time with a slightly different look, Dr. Ripper was to run a little freak show featuring characters very loosely based on the friends that I made in those dark dingy streets.
Finally in 2016 I revisited the sketchbook with all those strange little characters, and the result is the book you hold in your hands.
If you enjoy your visit, you share my love of
dark humour and I thank you.
If you're easily offended, put this book down
and go do some knitting.

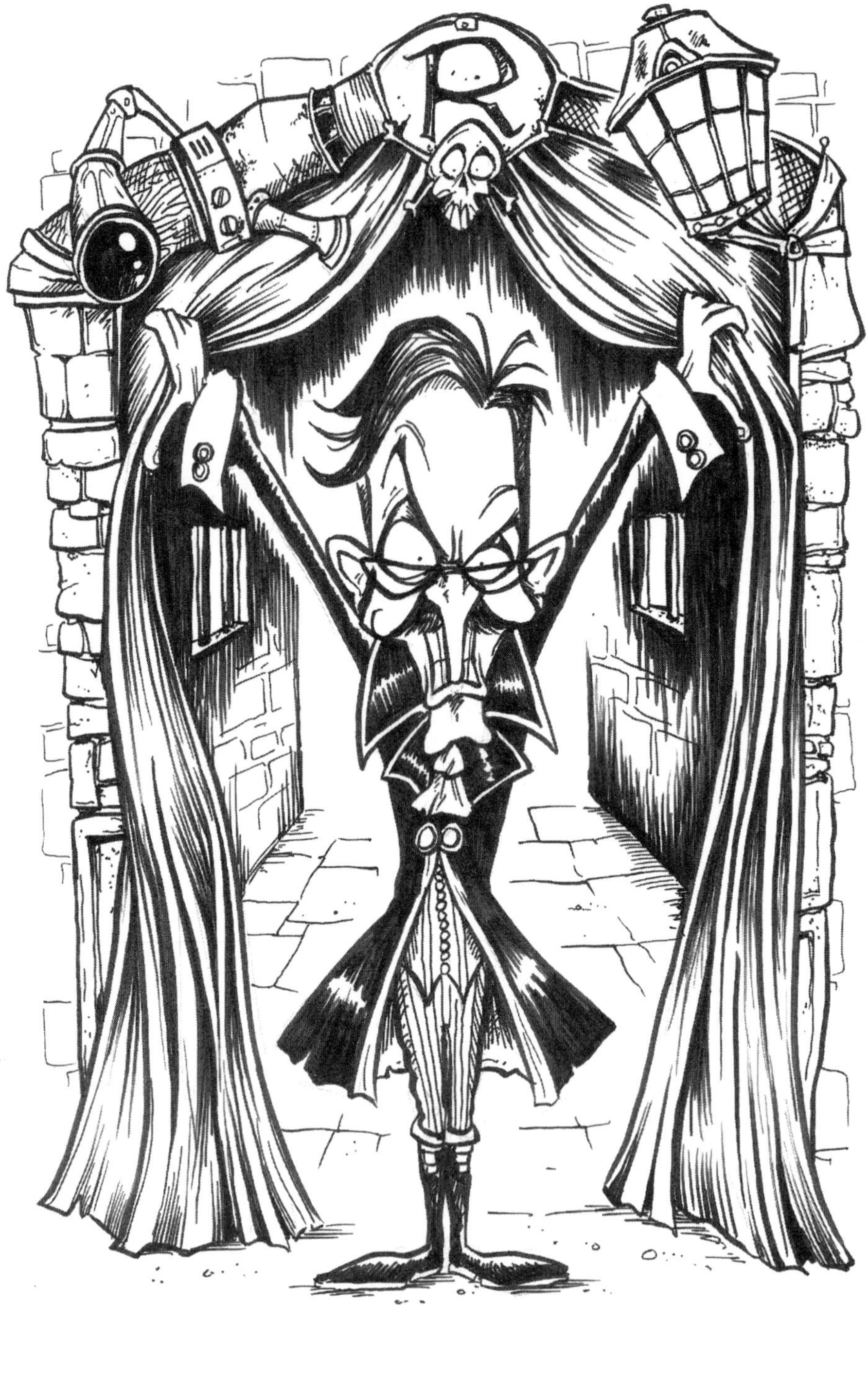
R

Introduction
by Dr J. Ripper

The correct way to start with any new meeting,
would be with a name and a friendly greeting.
So I'll start with my intro, all friendly and chipper,
with my name which is simply, Dr Jacob Ripper.

Greetings, dear humans, each and every one,
whether clever or stupid, depressing or fun.
I welcome you all to my carnival of odd,
devoid of good nature, abandoned by God.

For here you will find a strange new collection,
of weirdos and loonies in every direction.
The things that you'll see here will haunt you for weeks,
Welcome my friends to my
Fabricated Freaks!

SUGAR FIZZ
SYRUP
PICKLE EGGS
PIG JU
FAT LICA
POPCORN
BEEF BALLS
GUT GOBBLES
LARD CHEWS

Ashley & Michael Ponsonby-Carruthers,
The Strangely Obsessive Vanity Brothers

Many years ago men were quite simple,
they cared not for their looks, they ignored every pimple.
But with movies and fashion everything changed,
the men turned vain, they became quite deranged.

Far away from this madness there lived two fat gits,
who hated fashion, it gave them the shits.
They lived in a caravan on a cliff way up high,
where they gorged on cake, sweeties and pie.

They were rich and had goodies delivered by van,
and they lay side by side like sardines in a can.
But one day all this gorging sealed the boys fate,
their food it was poisoned and it was now too late.

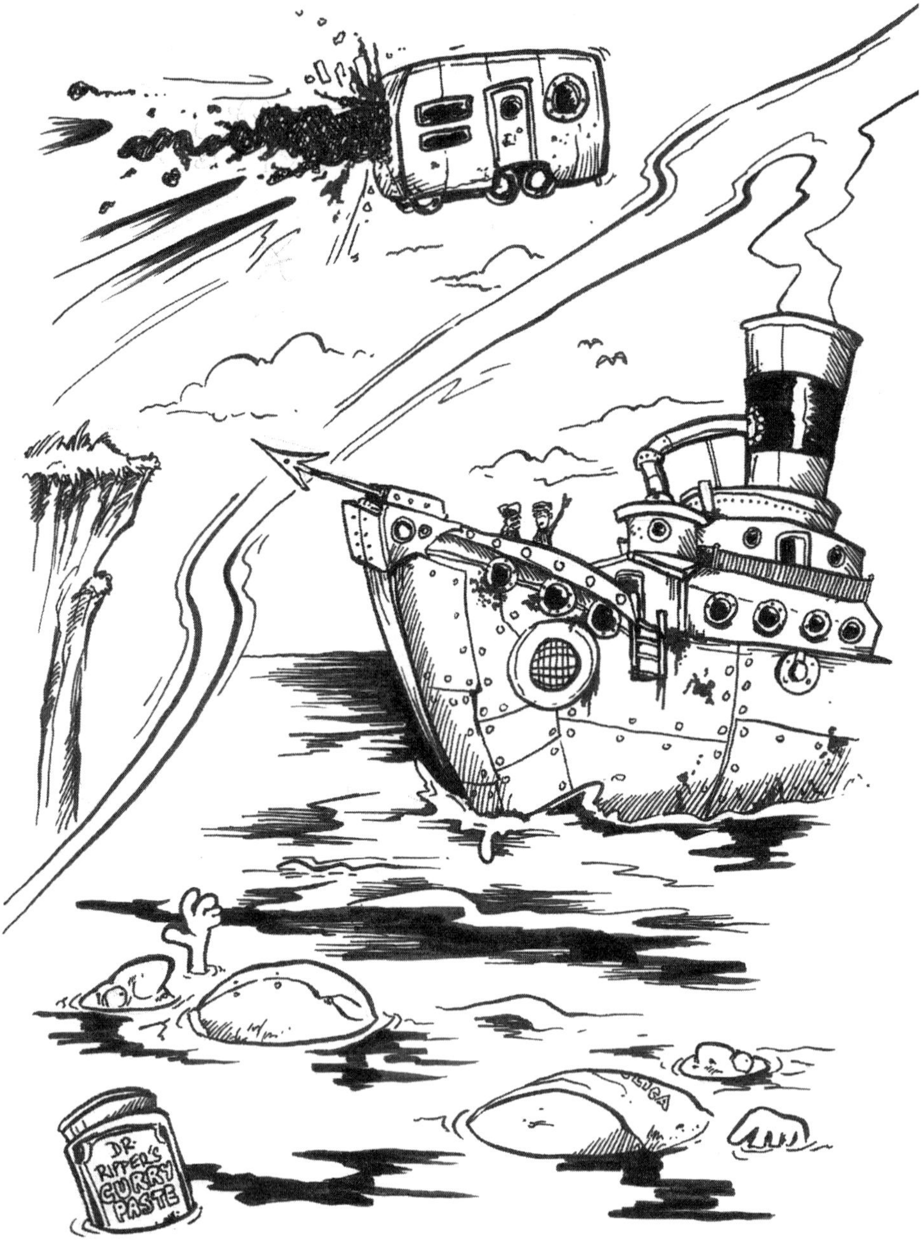
DR. RIPPER'S CURRY PASTE

Their stomachs rumbled, they did not know what to do,
and their home exploded in a volcano of poo.
The caravan took off with a violent motion,
and exploded into the middle of the ocean.

The caravan sunk but the brothers were bloated,
and up they popped to the surface and floated.
..and when things had gone so terribly wrong,
it was now that the whaling ship Doom came along.

Mistaking the brothers for blubbery whales,
the sailors aboard tried to harpoon their tails,
and with the harpoons having a firm grip,
the brothers were dragged onto the deck of the ship.

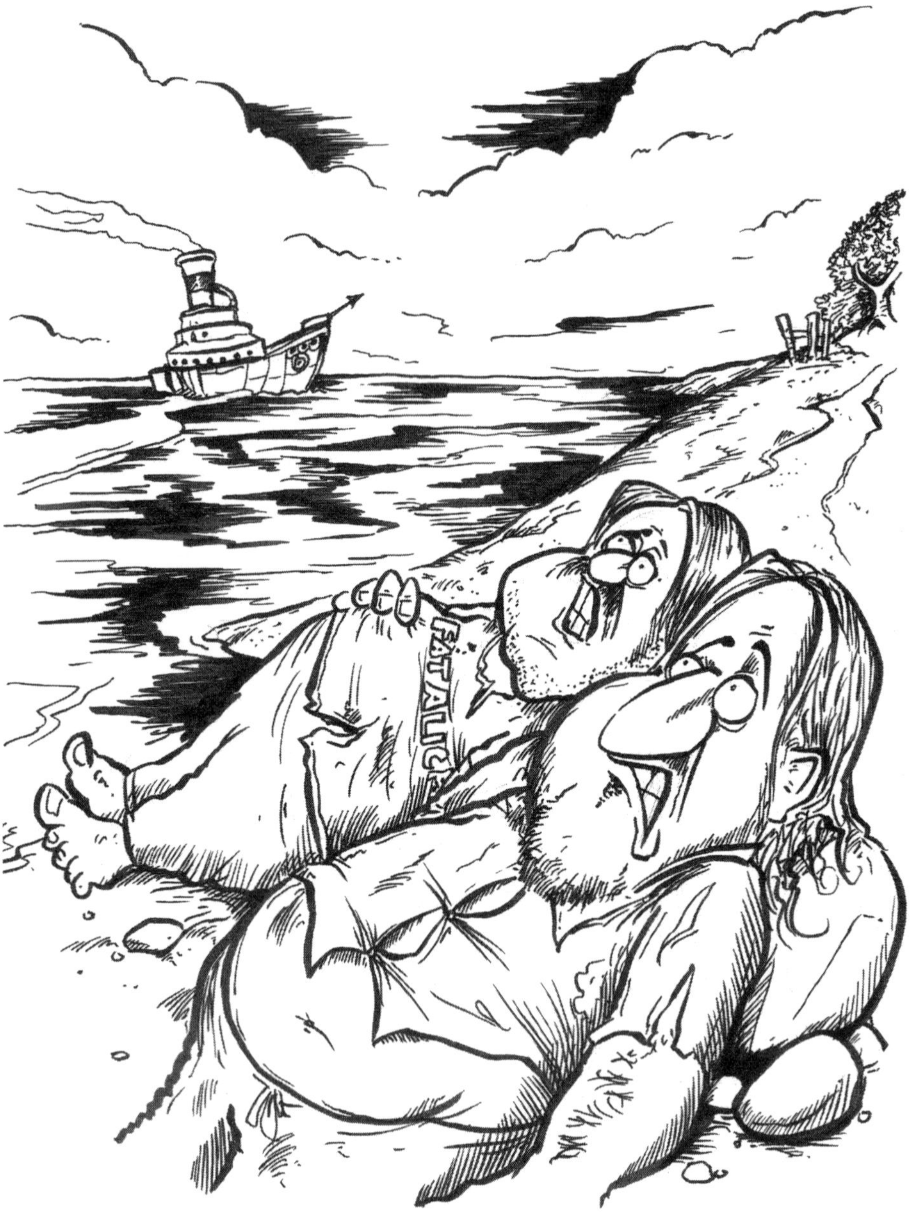
FATALICA

The captain said, "Men, you're losing your touch,
these are just blokes who've eaten too much!"
Realising their catch of the day was quite poor,
they left the fatties on a nearby shore.

So Ashley & Michael, the great big fat men,
decided to start their lives over again.
They went on diets, became slender and thin,
but their greed moved on to a new kind of sin.

Though eating quite healthy, the boys went insane,
even though now not greedy they're incredibly vain.
Fashion and grooming became their new infections,
and they spend all day now staring at their reflections.

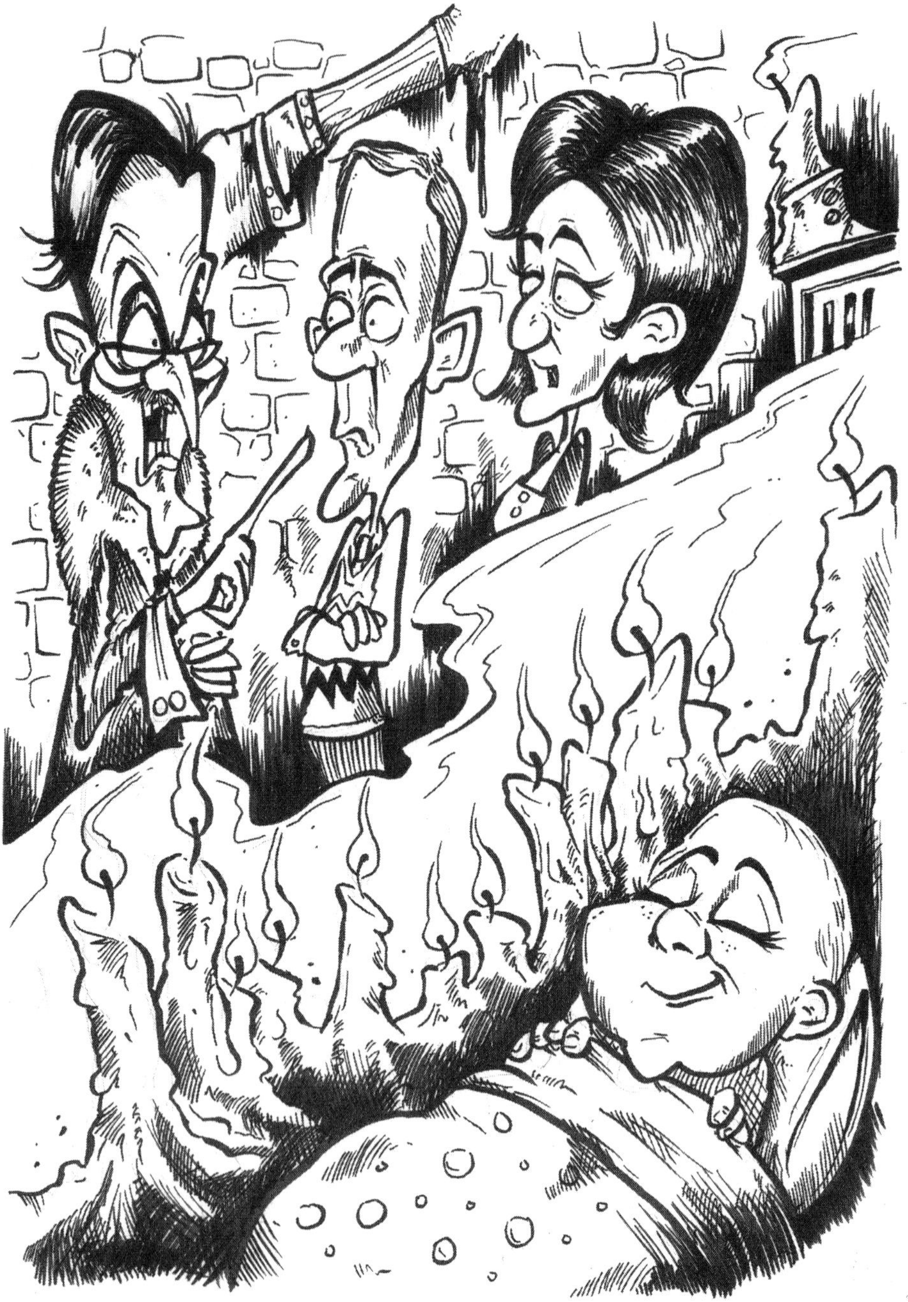

Cathryn Scarfe & the Murderous Laugh

There was a young couple all friendly and mild,
who desperately wanted to have their own child.
After doctors and tests and shagging for years,
there still was no baby and their eyes filled with tears.

Feeling so desperate with their broken hearts,
they turned to an expert in the black arts.
After lighting a candle and casting a spell,
he warned them they would have a child from hell.

The husband said, "We care not, where our child is from,
we'll give it so much love nothing can go wrong."
..and so soon the couple were blessed with a child,
and she didn't seem evil, she just lay there and smiled.

The girl they called Cathryn, and she made not one noise,
as she sat there each day and played with her toys.
..and as the girl got older, week after week,
the parents soon realised that she would not speak.

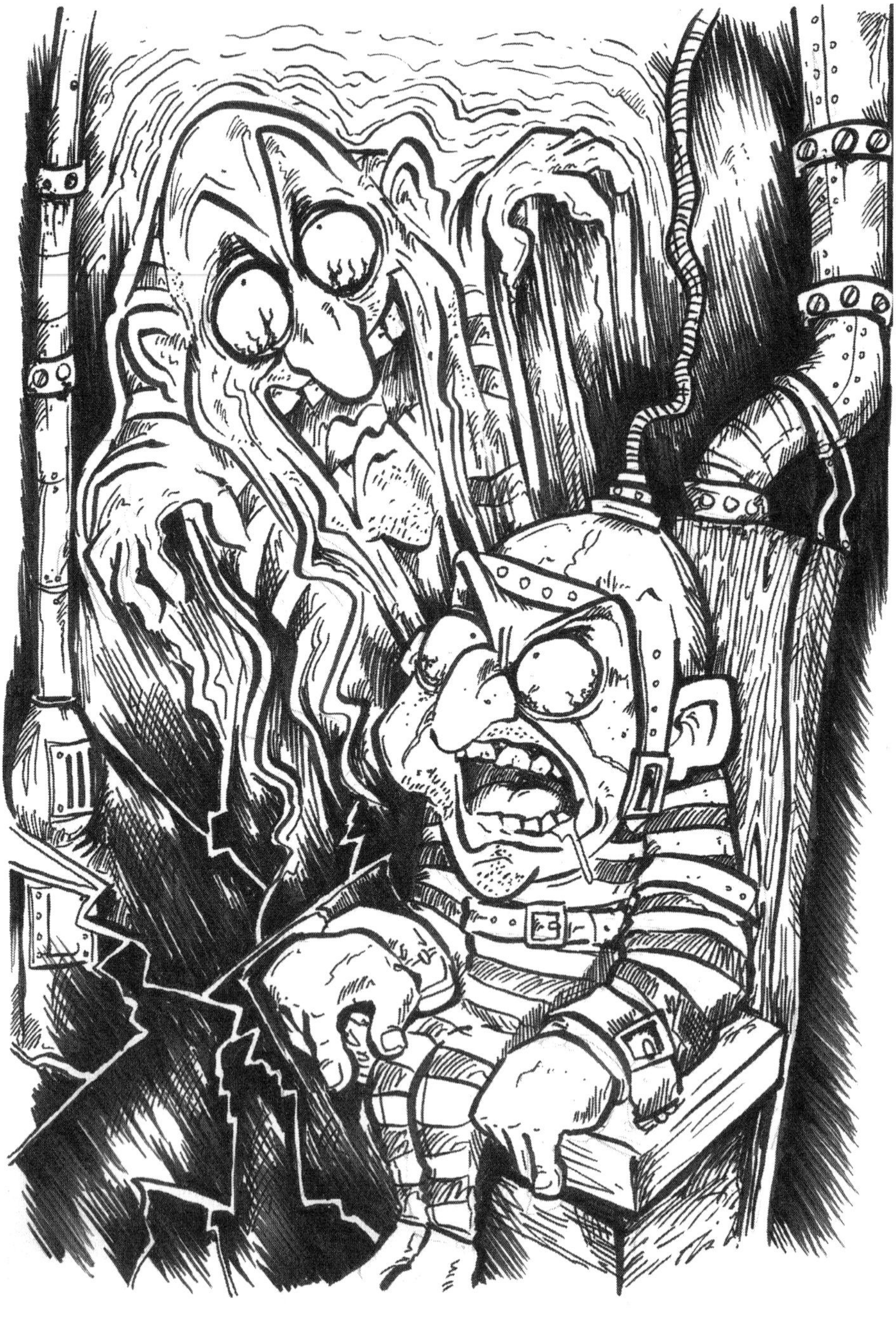

Years passed by and though there was no violence,
the parents became spooked by Cathryn's creepy silence.
By her 20th birthday she still hadn't spoken,
but this would be the day when the silence was broken..

Just a few miles away a murderer had risen,
to his final day in the old local prison.
No longer would this man make innocent blood flow,
or so he thought as he walked down death row.

Bernard the Bastard died in the electric chair,
and his evil ghost flew out into the air.
Desperate to live though his body was dead,
his spirit took refuge inside Cathryn's head.

So why may you ask, did this dead evil sod,
pick Cathryn, it might seem to you rather odd.
But Cathryn's curse if you will now please note,
was that she was inflicted with a demonic throat.

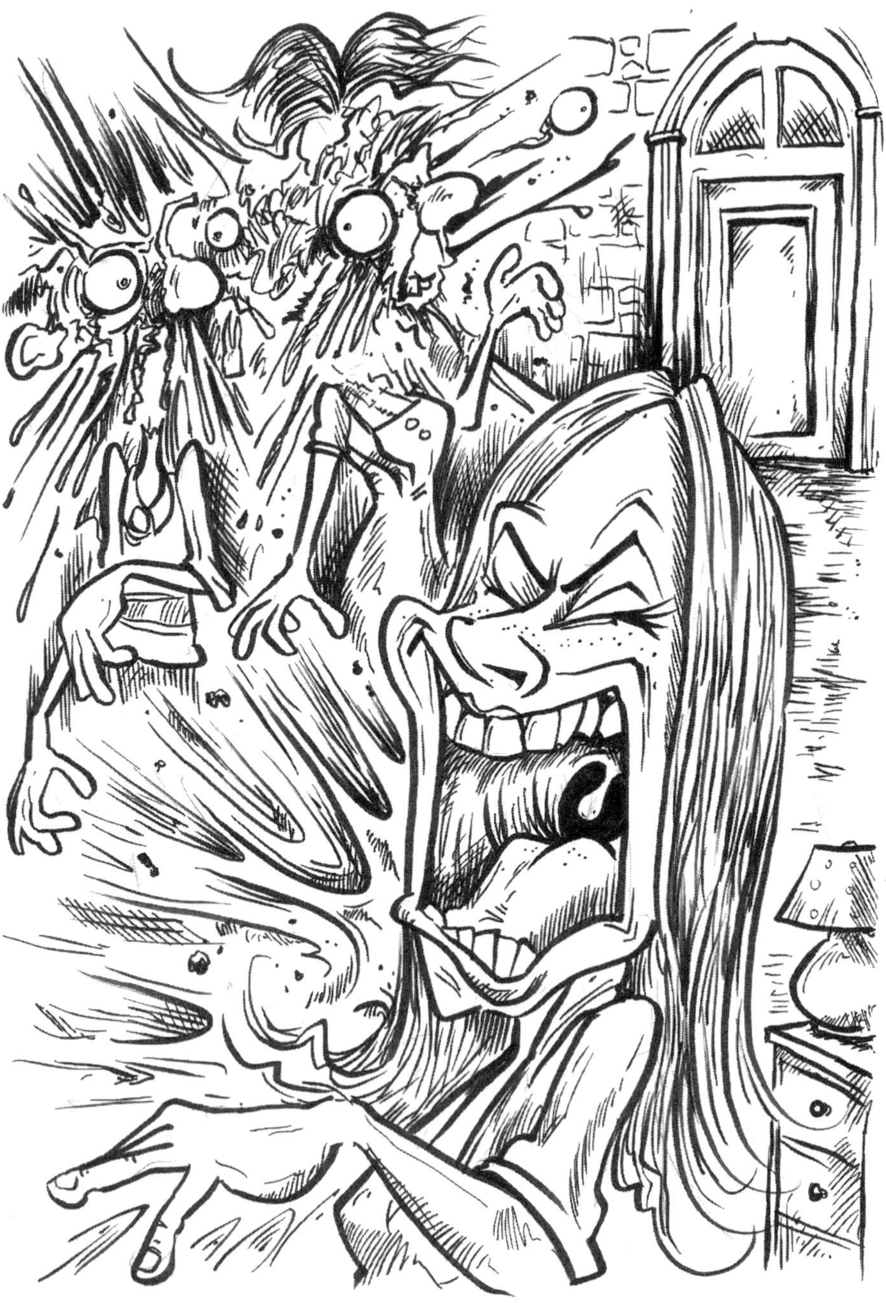

Feeling more power than he'd ever had,
Bernard seized the tonsils that were so very bad.
The tonsils were his, he now had them tackled,
and Cathryn's head simply fell back.. and she cackled.

As they stared at their daughter, the parents looked shocked,
as the laughter grew louder, the house shook and rocked,
the noise just got louder, 'til their heads overloaded,
and finally mum and dad's heads just exploded.

But don't worry, for Bernard can no longer cause pain,
for although a ghost, he is locked up again.
He's inside Cathryn's head and now she cannot laugh,
as she's gagged with a big re-enforced chain-mail scarf.

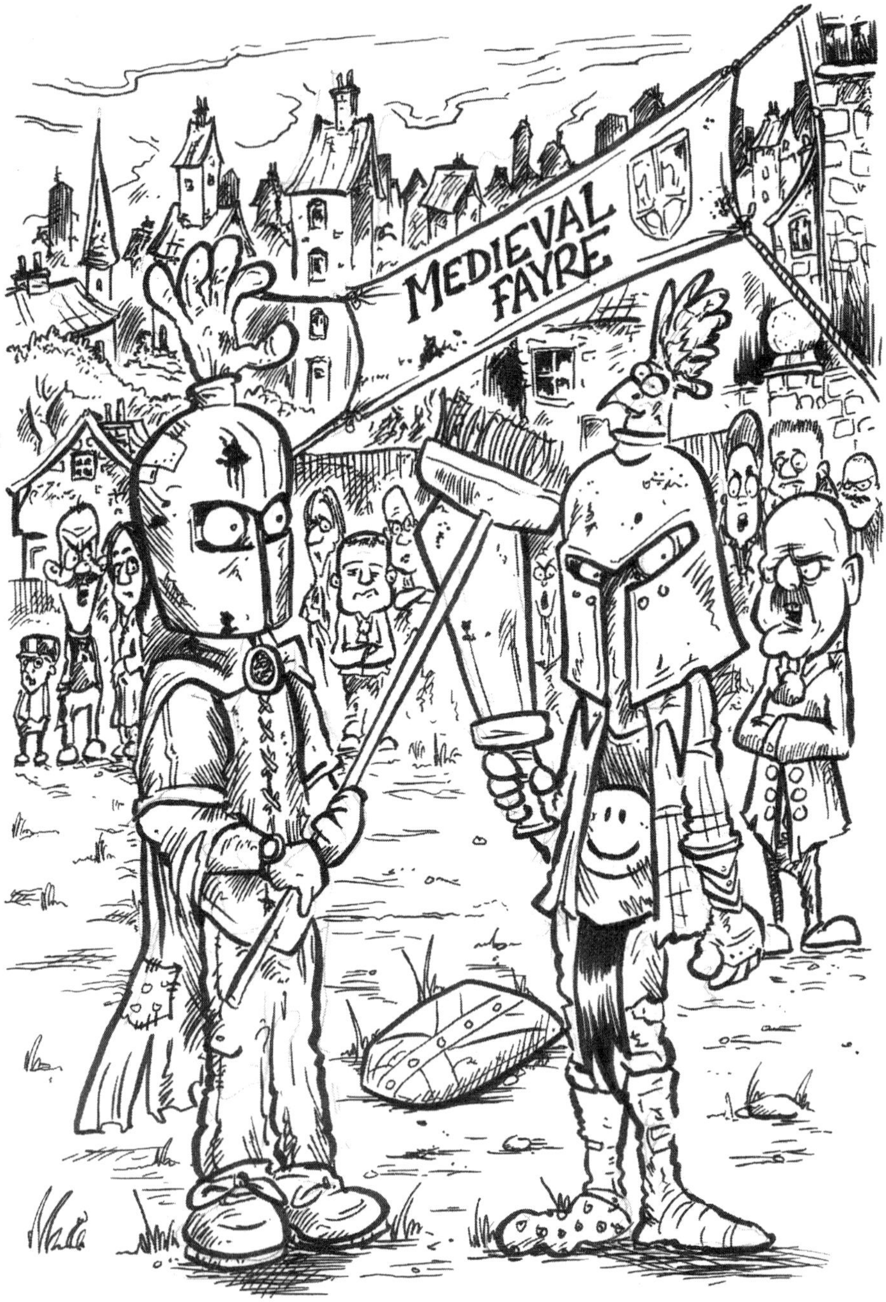
MEDIEVAL FAYRE

The Sad Strange Tale of a man named Ned,
Impaled on a Sword and he should be Dead

Summer in the city and excitement filled the air,
for that was the time of the medieval fair,
and the noise was loud but would get quiet and calmer,
when it was time for the knights in their shining armour.

One year sadly the budget had shrunk,
and to put it bluntly the costumes stunk.
As the knights fought, people started to mock,
when they'd spot a t-shirt or a modern day sock.

"What rot, what crap, how poor, how shite!"
the crowds did shout while they watched the fight.
But suddenly the jeers turned into silence,
when up stepped Ned, the black Knight of Violence.

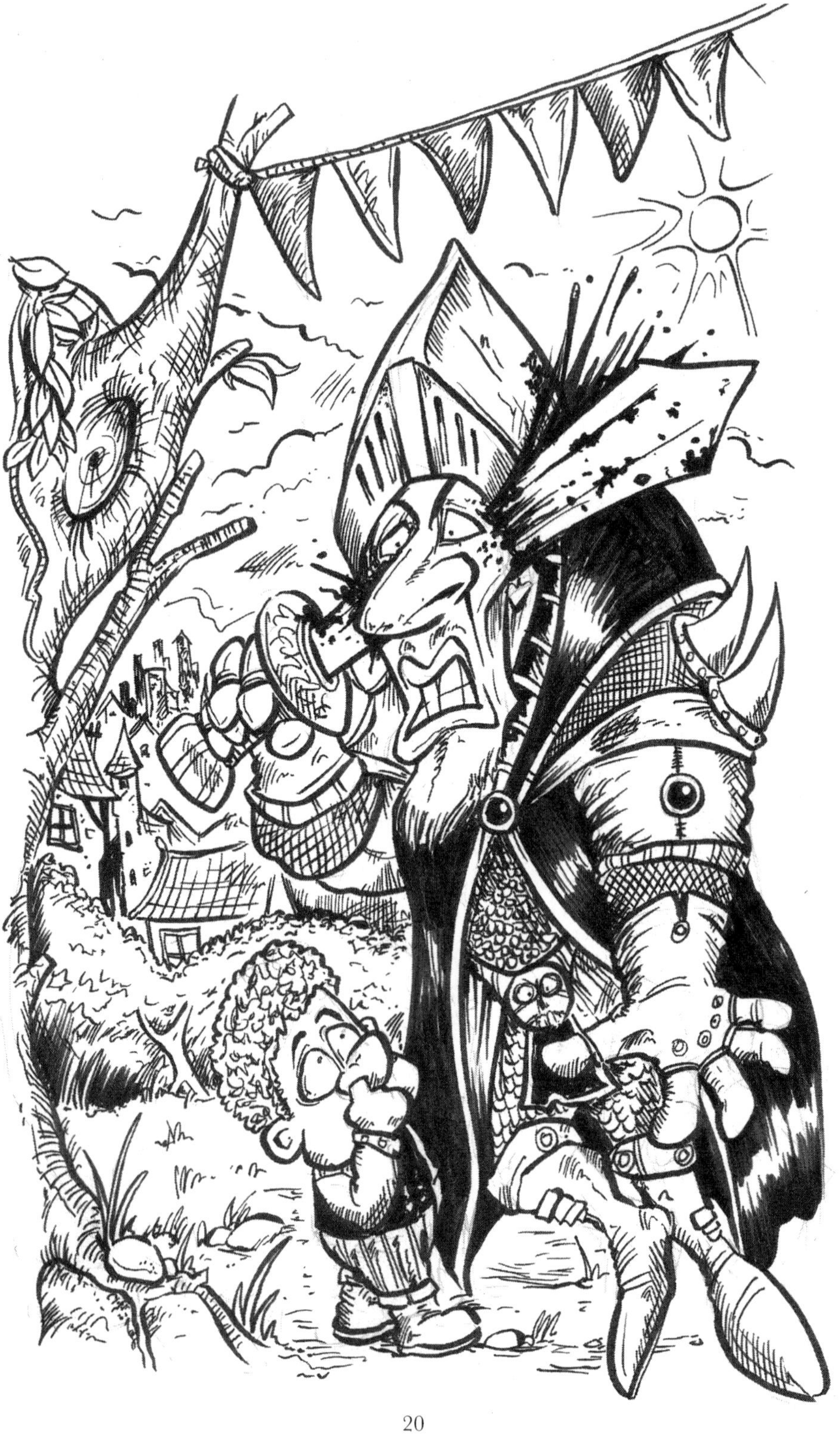

Re-inactment was Ned's only passion,
and he put his own money into knight fashion.
His gleaming costume made the crowd applaud,
and not only that, he was good with a sword.

Ned had mastered the weapon he carried,
as he swung and he leapt and he thrust and he parried.
His amazing technique drove the crowd wild,
but Ned's luck went downhill when up stepped a child.

So very impressed with Ned's great swordplay,
this stupid small child simply stepped in the way,
and despite the manoeuvres and talents of Ned,
he avoided the child but impaled his own head.

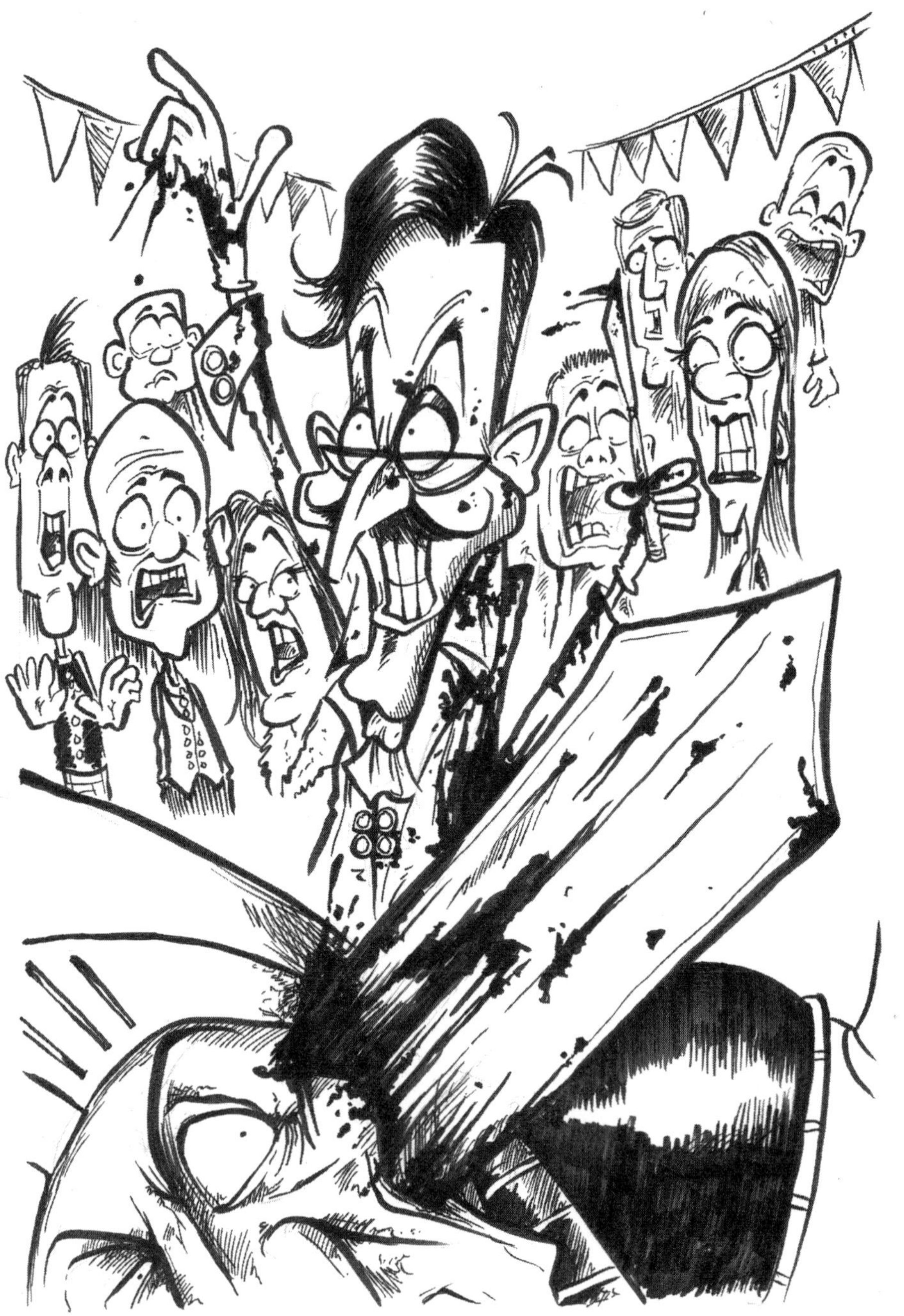

The crowd started screaming, some were even sick,
but then up ran a surgeon who had to think quick.
He pulled out a scalpel, a needle and thread,
surely it was too late, the man must be dead.

After an hour, Ned let out a cough,
and the surgeon stood and held his hands aloft.
"Don't worry my friends, though the sword's still stuck fast,
I've saved dear Ned's life!" .. and with that he laughed.

So miraculously, the Black Knight still lives,
and now it's a different performance he gives.
For now he just stands there, which might seem quite dull,
were it not for that sword sticking out of his skull.

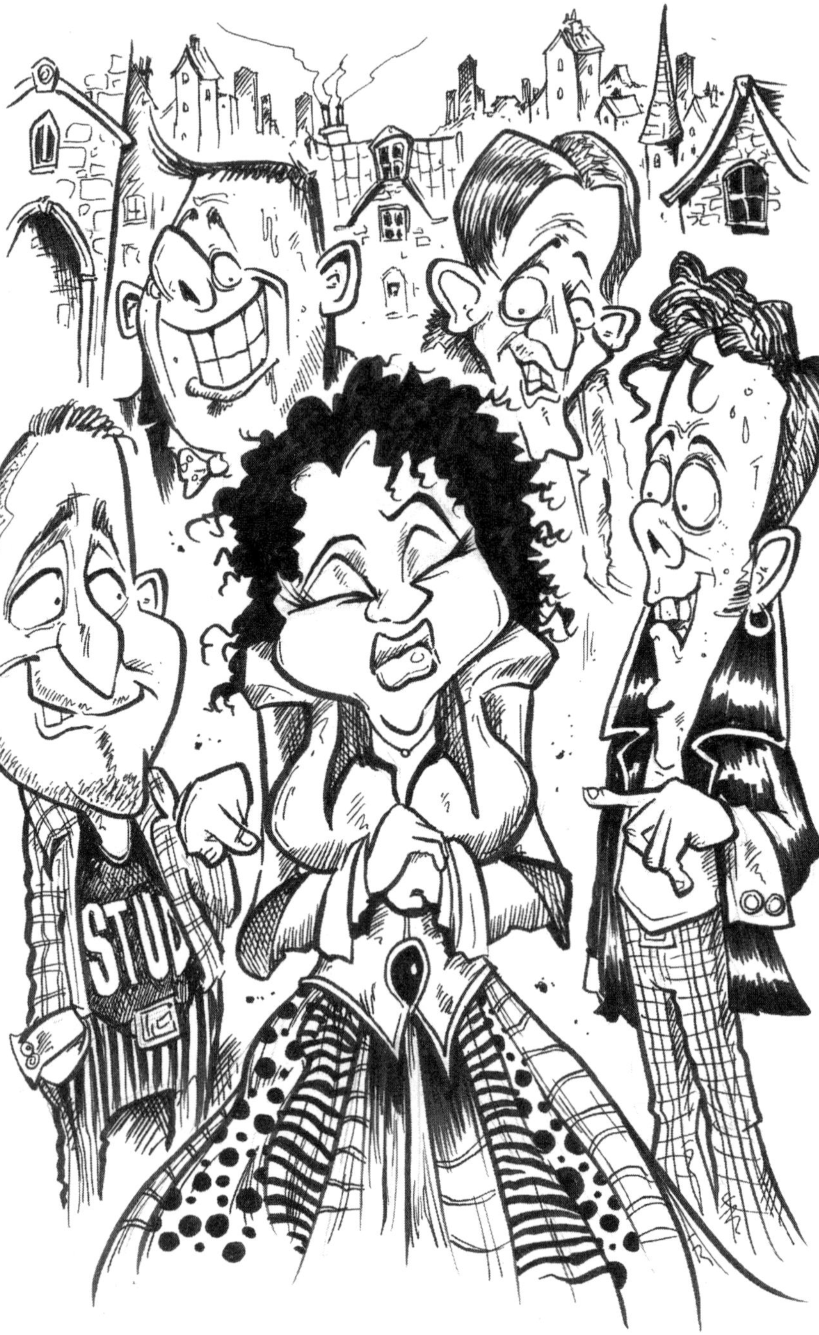

*Claire von Peavage
and the Violent Cleavage*

One of those things that is so hard to gauge,
is how a girl will react when she's coming of age.
But teenage girls reading this should beware,
the sad strange story of a girl named Claire.

As a girl, Claire was quiet and life was quite easy,
but as she got older things began to turn sleazy.
For as she reached her late teens she began to get curvy,
and oddly enough all the boys became pervy.

Pretty soon she was sick of all the boys staring,
but she simply kept quiet as she wasn't that daring.
As time went on though, Claire could no longer cope,
because the greasy boys fingers had started to grope.

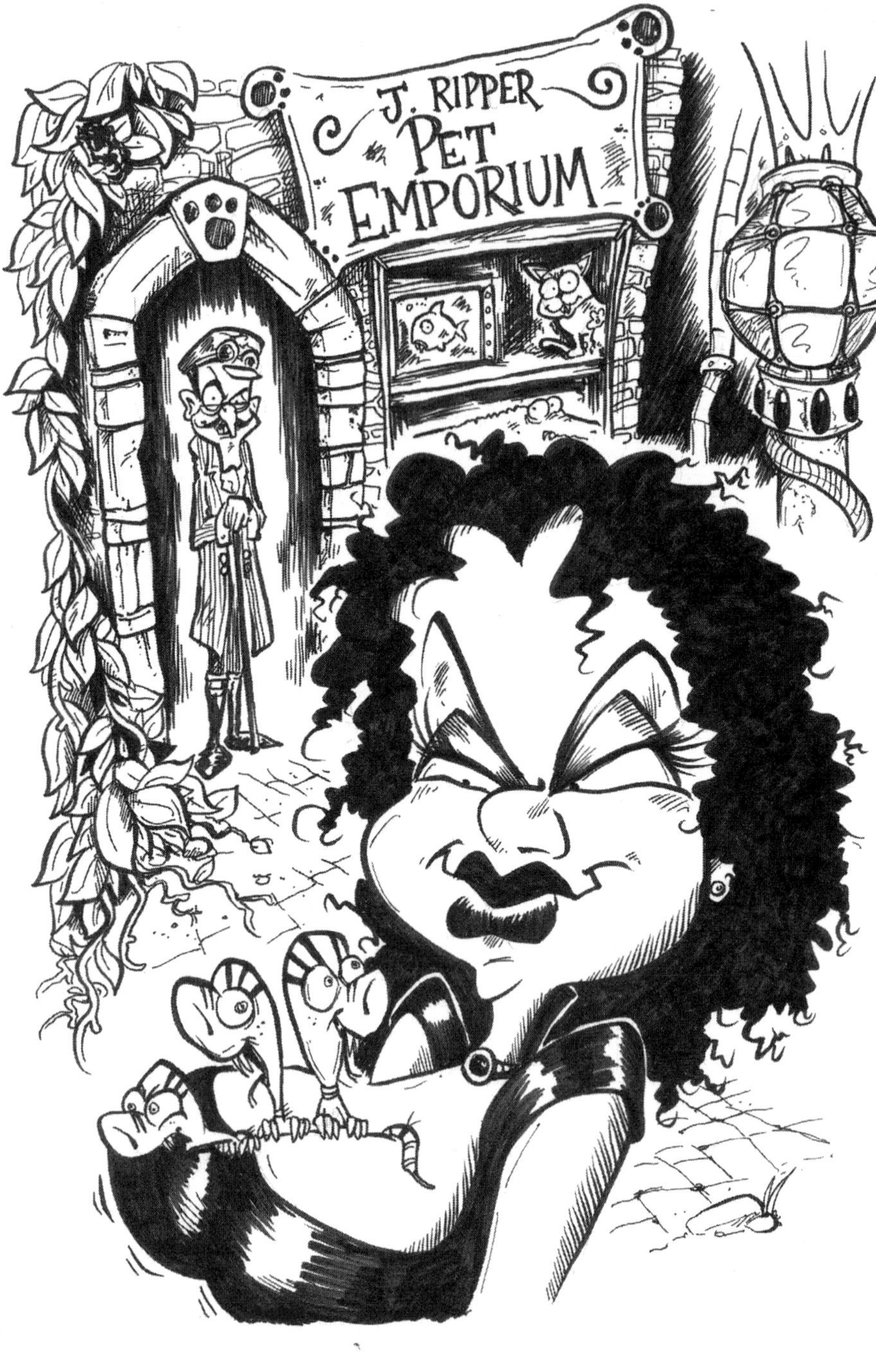
J. RIPPER
PET
EMPORIUM

Tired of filthy fingers creeping down her top,
Claire formed a plan and went to the pet shop.
She bought some strange lizards from the Far East,
called the Venomous Red Kamikaze Beast.

So with months of training with small meaty bits,
she trained the meat eating lizards to nest in her tits.
Then in a small top revealing her wares,
she would have revenge on those boys and their stares.

With a big saucy smile, while wobbling her curves,
she approached Big Dave, the King of the Pervs.
"Hello there Dave," she said, "Fancy a squeeze?"
and Dave started to dribble and just said, "Yes, please!"

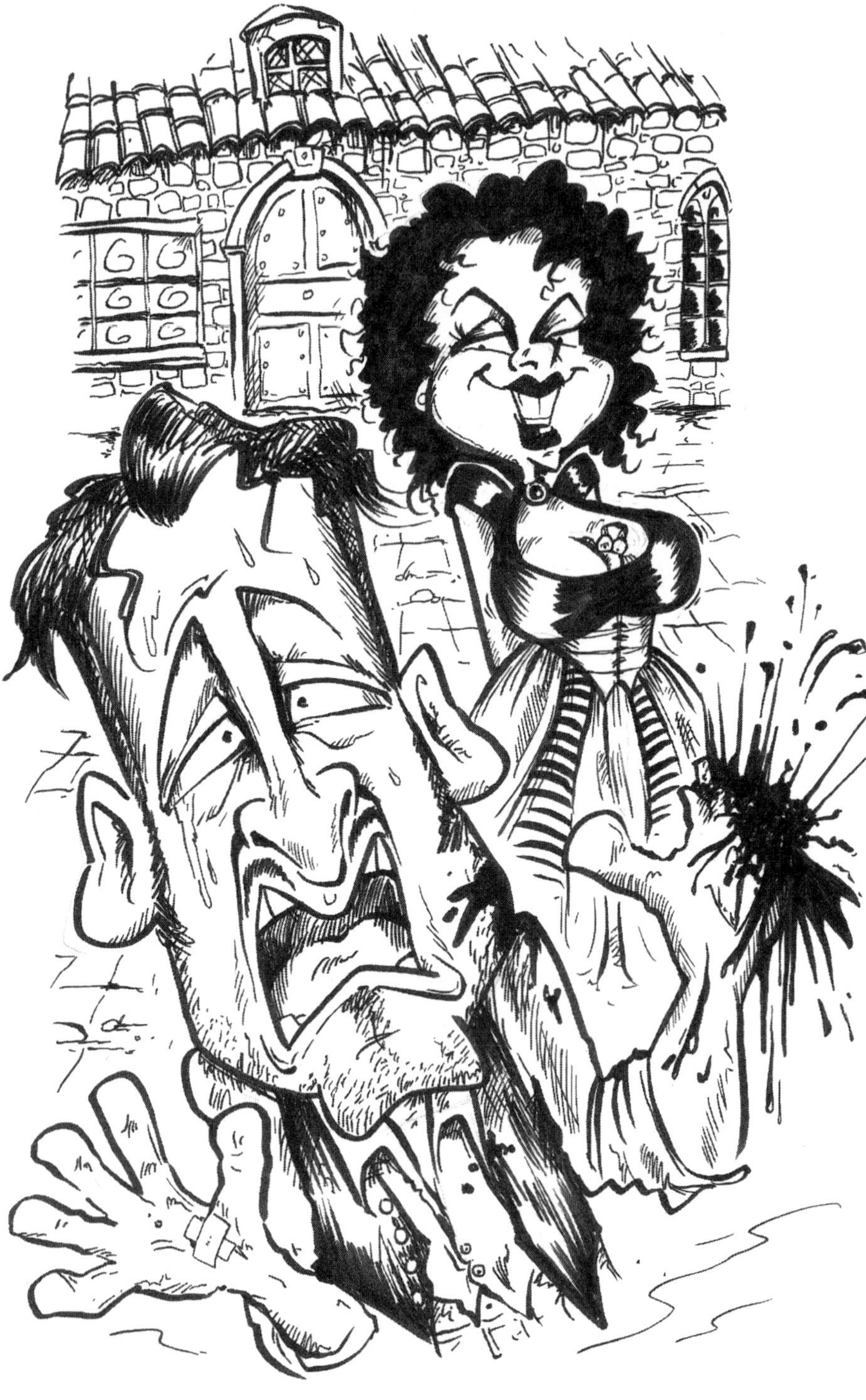

This boob burglar was the worst of all felons,
as he thrust his fat fingers between those big melons.
Claire smiled then laughed as Dave started to yell,
as his fingers were eaten, the plan had worked well.

So as time went on, men soon learned the curse,
if you went near Claire, you'd lose fingers.. or worse!
and Claire found the lizards so very handy,
.. until one day when she began to get randy.

So even though now Claire has boobs nice and large,
no men will come near her as the lizards are in charge,
and now in her twenties, Claire is feeling grumpy,
wanting some affection or some rumpy-pumpy.

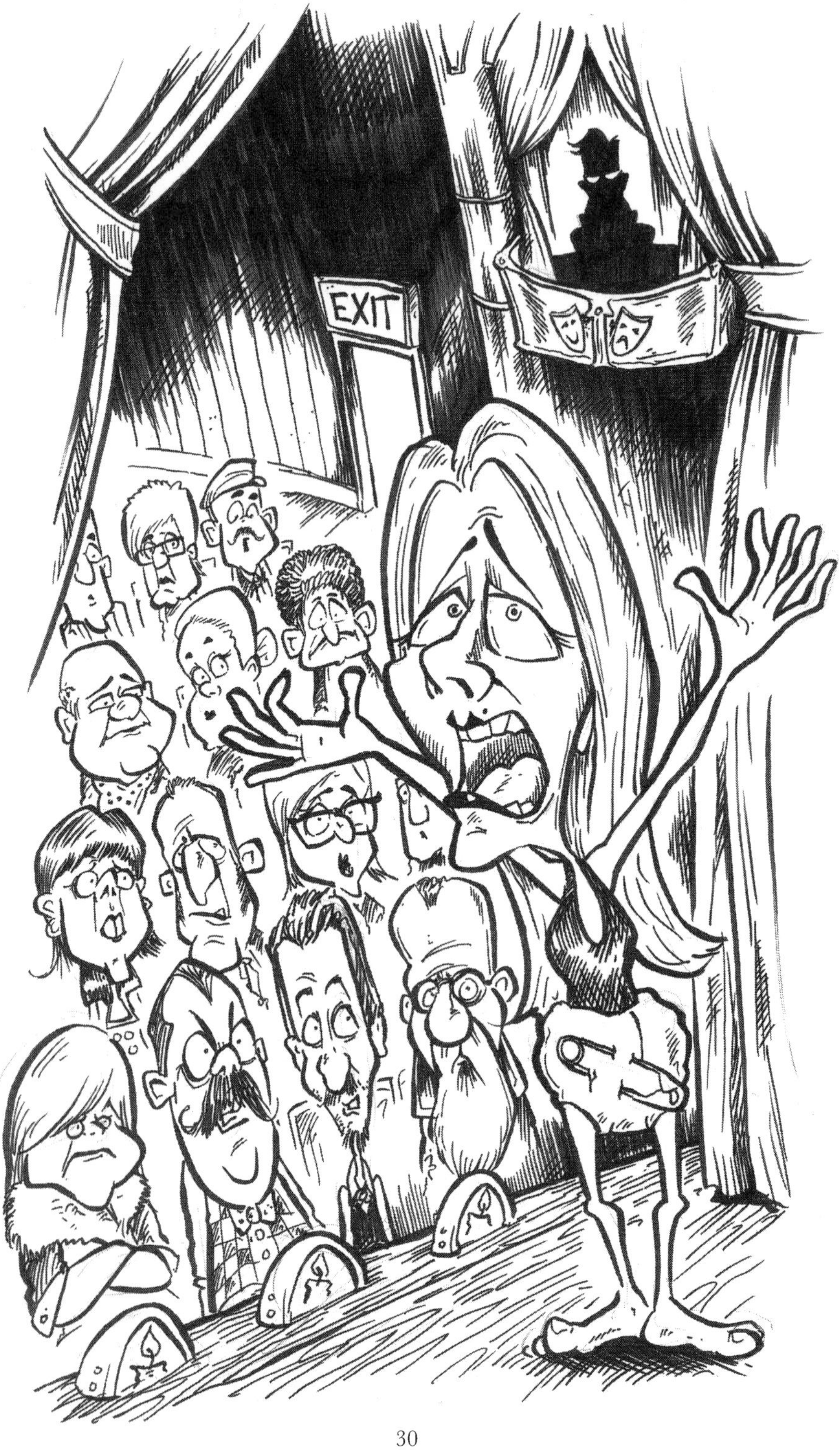
EXIT

Natalie Fontaine,
She's Purely Insane

Over in Pity City's West End,
Opera was once a popular trend,
and of all of the opera stars on stage,
Natalie Fontaine was all of the rage.

Although of a stature reasonably small,
her opera singing was so powerful,
and Natalie's fame was set to grow,
until she starred in a disastrous show.

The show was called "Waaagh!" and it was a bit crappy,
she had to scream like a baby whilst wearing a nappy.
It was a comedy opera that was supposed to be quirky,
but sadly the crowds thought it was a bit of a turkey.

Due to bad reviews that started to leak,
the show had shut down within just a week.
So poor Nat felt understandably bitter,
as her great reputation went straight down the shitter.

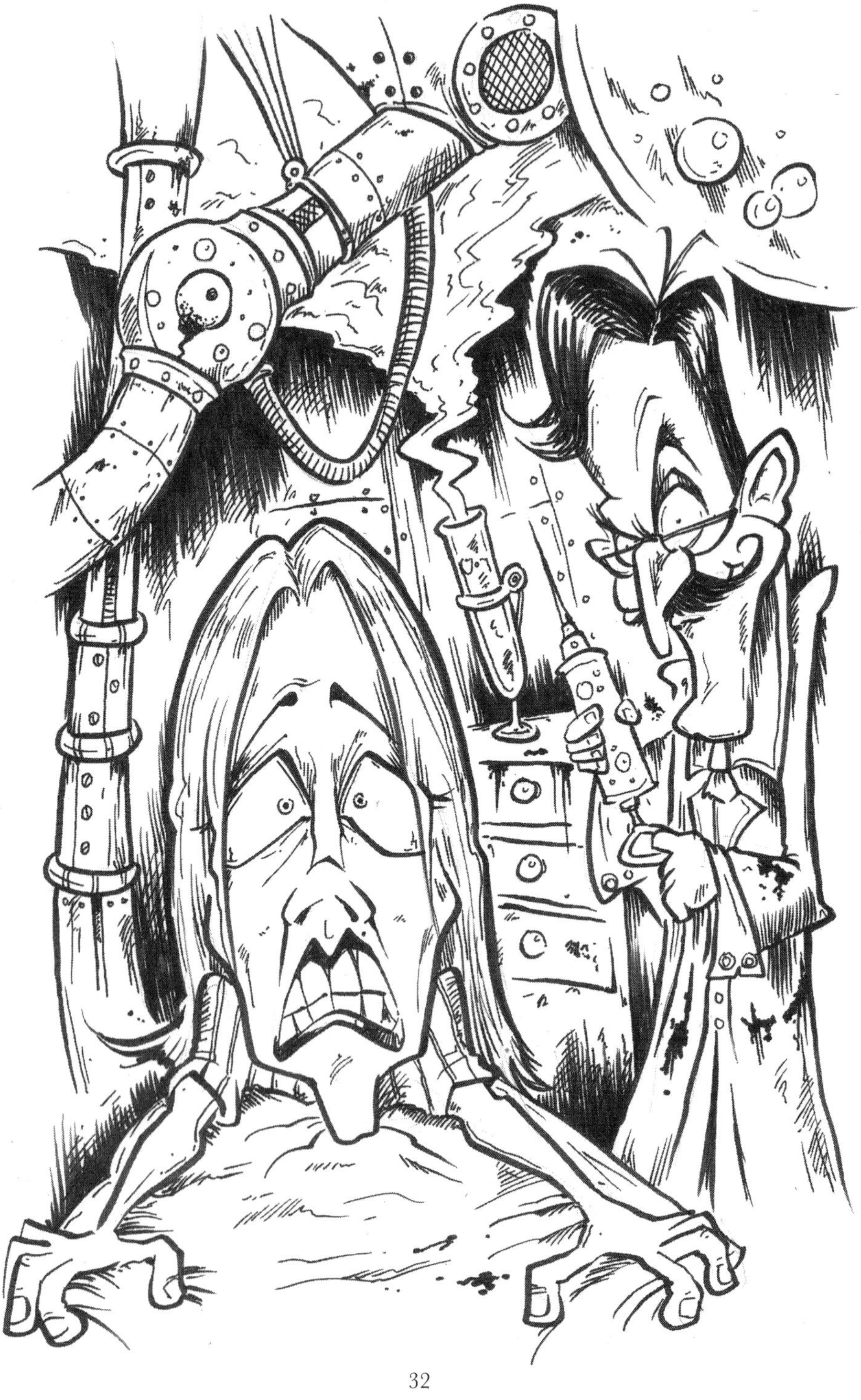

As the weeks went by, the girl became poor,
and she couldn't afford to pay bills any more.
But Nat was quite strong and in her defiance,
for money she gave in to medical science.

A lab down the road claimed to combat infections,
and were testing out all kinds of strange new injections.
After getting some cash of a rather small sum,
the scientist injected poor Nat in the bum.

As Natalie yelled, the strange scientist smiled,
for he'd done something naughty, something pretty wild.
The injection she'd had was a curious mix,
of the DNA of 3000 crazed lunatics.

All of the logic and sanity of Nat,
were gone in just seconds, simply like that!
Nat laughed and she span and she screamed up a storm,
for now she was insanity in it's purest form.

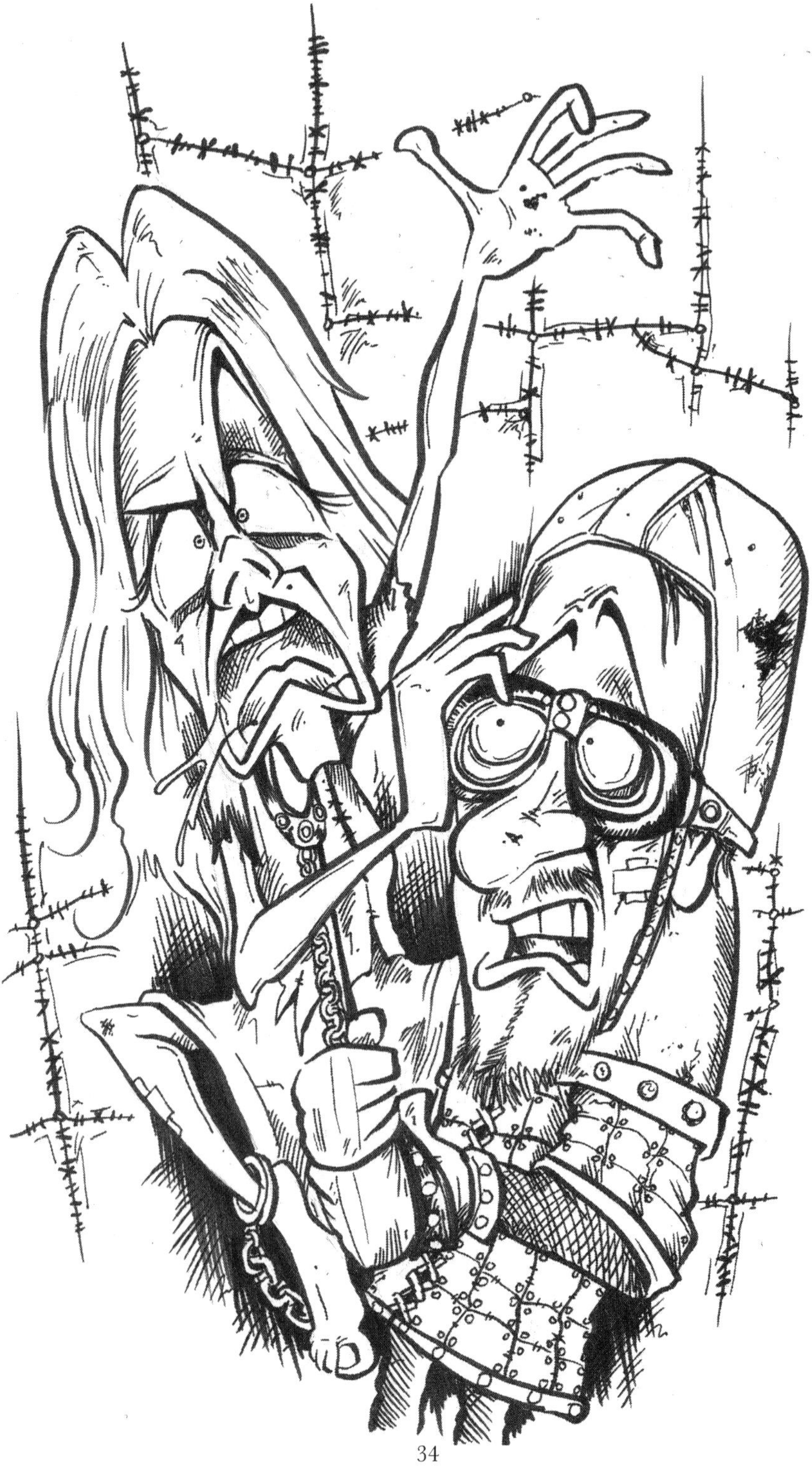

The scientist then took her to a sinister young man,
a crazed lad called Jon who was her biggest fan.
As the reason for this new madness she'd got,
was because she was part of a sinister plot!

For Jon was an obsessive opera groupie,
who'd begged the scientist to make poor Nat go loopy.
So now that Nat's mind had completely depleted,
she could not tell people how she'd been so cheated.

"Haha!" laughed Jon, giving the scientist cash,
"Some people may say that my methods are rash,
I may now have spent all of my wealth,
but I've got Nat Fontaine all to myself!"

But things weren't so great for this obsessed boy,
for danger came from having Nat as a toy,
now beaten and bloody Jon has now got the role,
of keeping that loony under control!

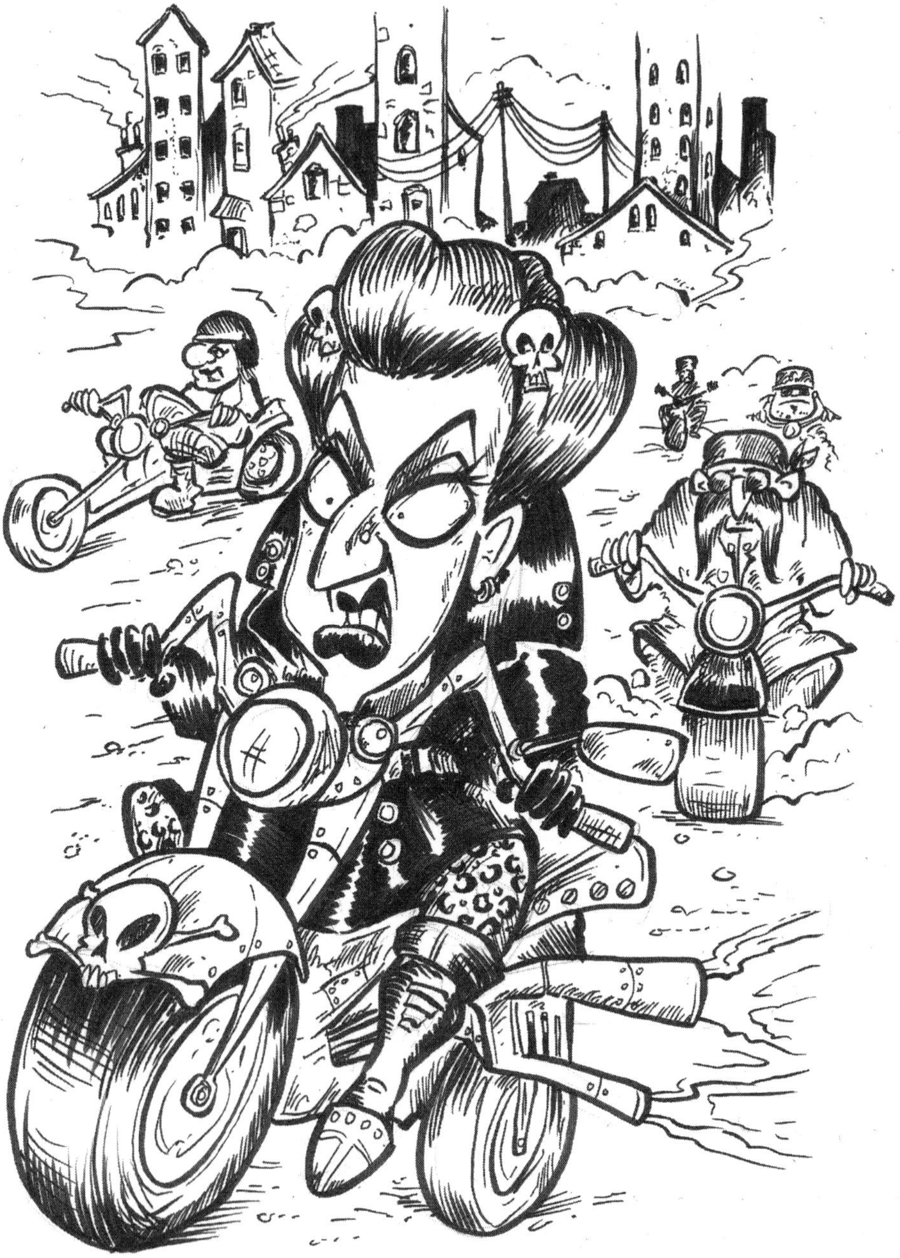

Lauren Hellbound
and the Nasty Nose Hound

Once a curse on the city was a group of bikers,
who attacked all the drivers, cyclists and hikers.
There was no woman, child or man,
who was safe from the wicked Hellbound clan.

Running the clan was a nasty mean pair,
nicknamed Poison Frog and Grizzly Bear.
Every day they loved to slaughter,
but the most wicked of all was Lauren their daughter

Like a monster her bike would tear up the street,
and she'd knock passers-by right off of their feet.
She'd break their bones and dance on their head,
and long before she was finished they'd pray to be dead.

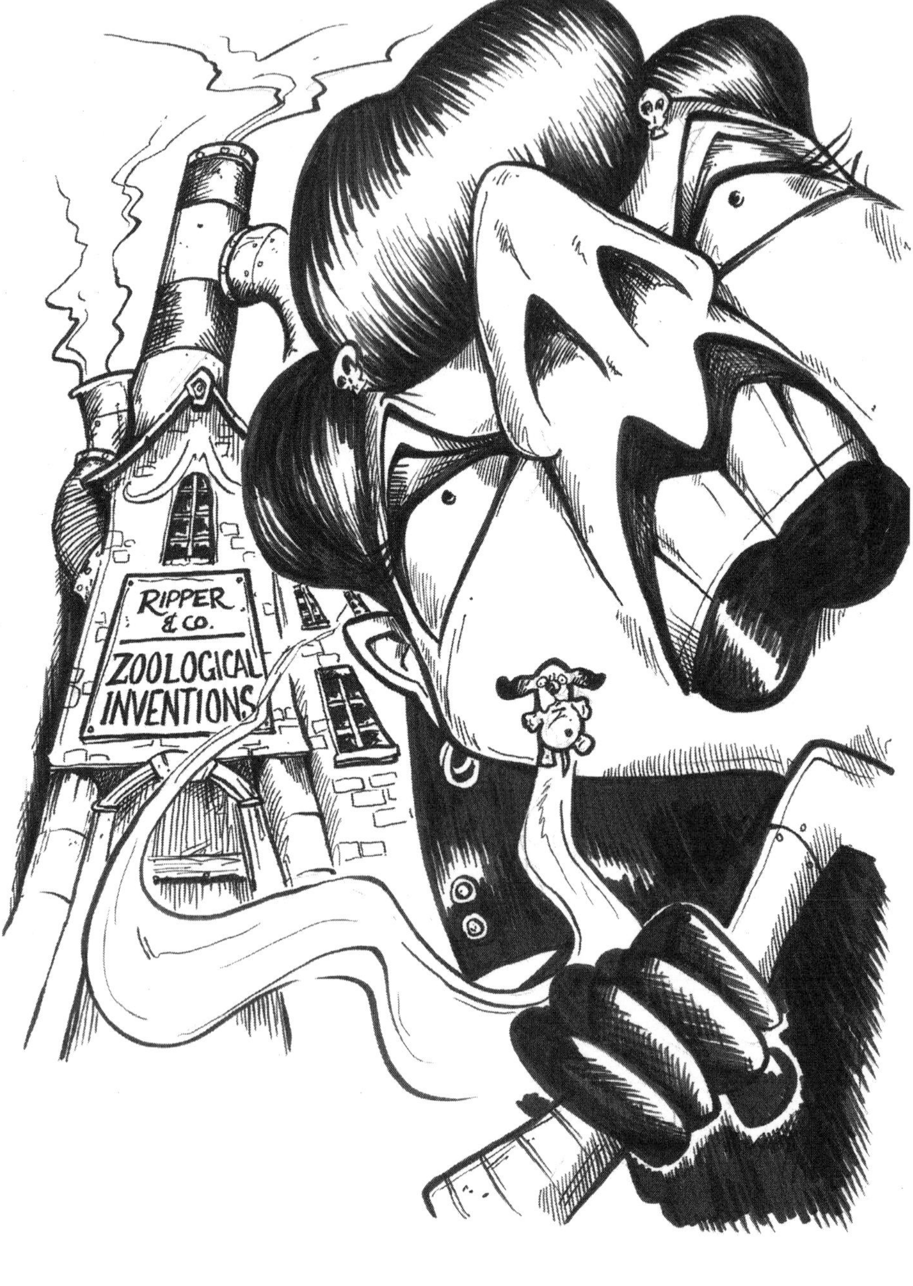
RIPPER
& CO.
ZOOLOGICAL
INVENTIONS

But one day she ended all of this molesting,
when the gang passed a building that did animal testing.
The worlds smallest dog had escaped from that place,
and it flew through the air and hit Lauren's face.

But she couldn't feel it and now I'll tell you why,
because this tiny dog was smaller than a fly!
It had shrunk thanks to drugs taken earlier that day,
and it crawled up her nose and decided to stay.

By now the gang's crimes were getting well known,
and the police force that chased them had suddenly grown.
..and while hiding out in a building that night,
it was now that the nose-hound started to bite!

The dog was quite vicious and as it scratched and bit,
Lauren jumped up like she was having a fit.
"Fnee!", shouted Lauren, "Fnee! Fnoooo!"
the gang became frantic, they didn't know what to do.

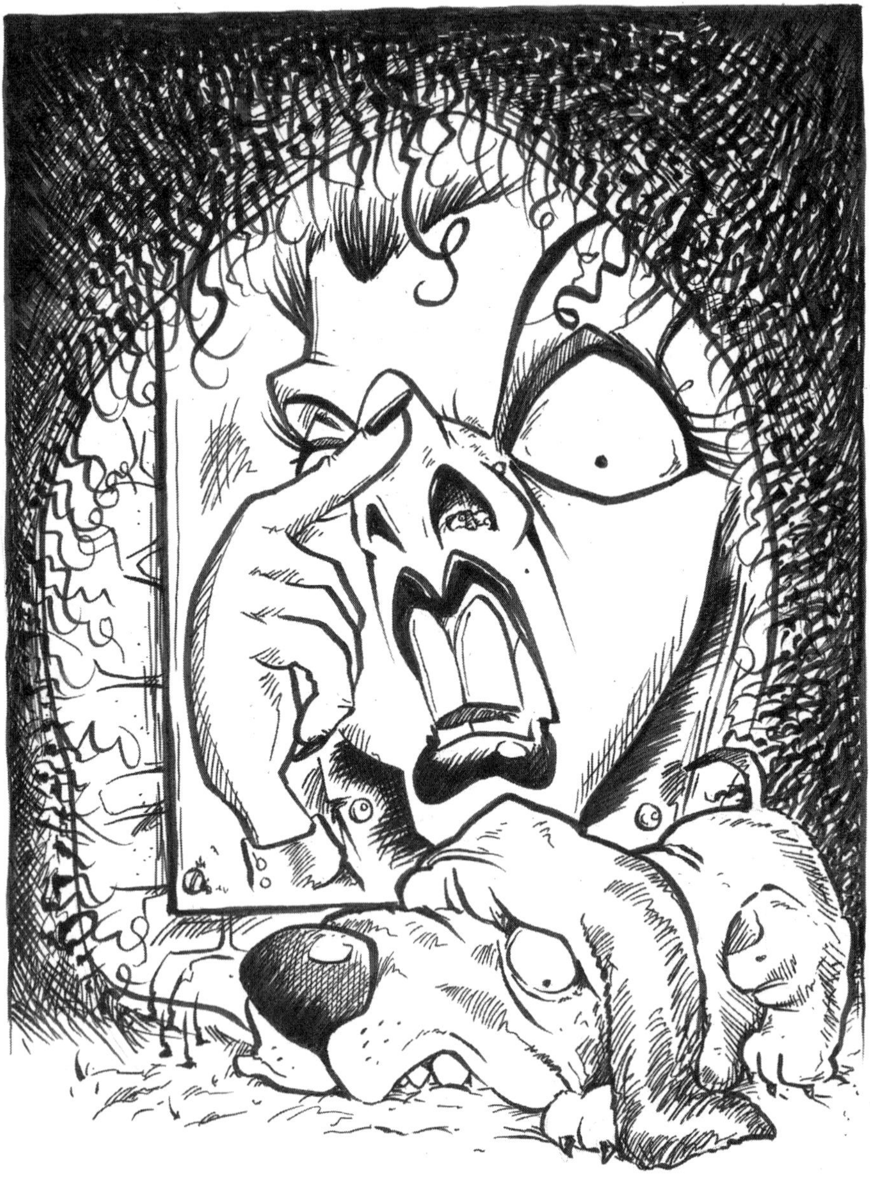

The police were close by, she could give them away,
they needed to go and they could not delay!
They said, "We'll be hung! ..and that we don't like!"
So they then buggered off, ..once they'd smashed up her bike.

She'd now been abandoned, she couldn't believe it,
and for some strange reason, she kept smelling dog shit.
So the weird psycho who had now been ditched,
made more nasal noises the more her nose itched.

By use of a mirror she discovered the cause,
that mean little hound that hung on with it's claws.
No matter how much she'd poke, sneeze and cough,
that strange little canine just would not piss off.

So now that the nose-hound refuses to go,
Lauren hides from the law in my little freak show,
and when the small dog begins to scratch around,
Lauren lets out that strange nasal sound.

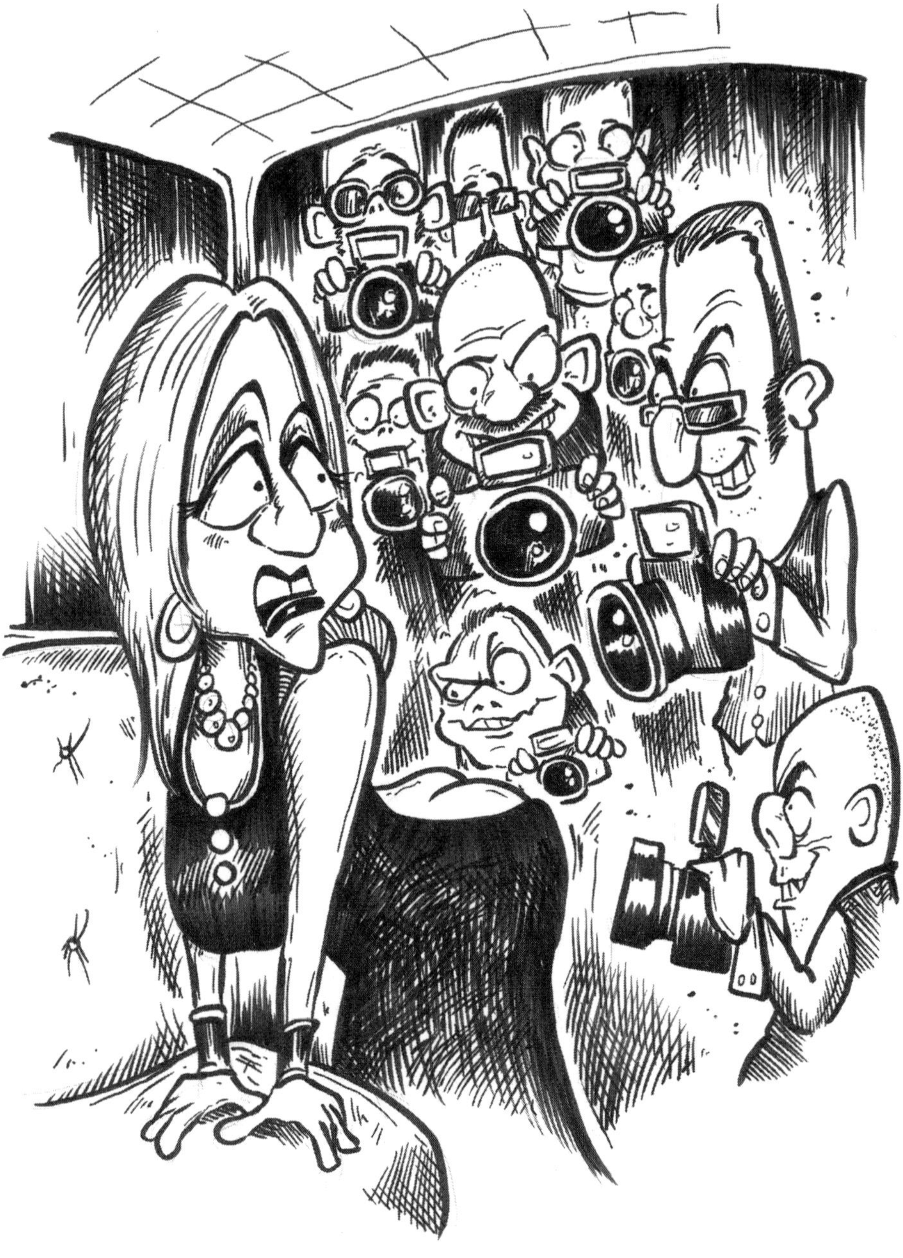

Lizzie Embrace
and her Bum for a Face

High on the hills of Pity City,
was a town devoted to celebrity.
This was the golden town of Glitch,
a haven for the famous and rich.

The most famous girl in this wondrous place,
was a movie star called Lizzie Embrace,
Lizzie dined and mixed with the a-list stars,
and frequented the poshest bars.

Even though young Liz was the toast of the town,
she began to wear the slightest frown,
for although her life should be free of stress,
she was hounded by the city's press.

One night the press went way too far,
when Liz climbed into a waiting car.
She wore a dress with a low-cut back,
and as she climbed in she revealed her butt-crack!

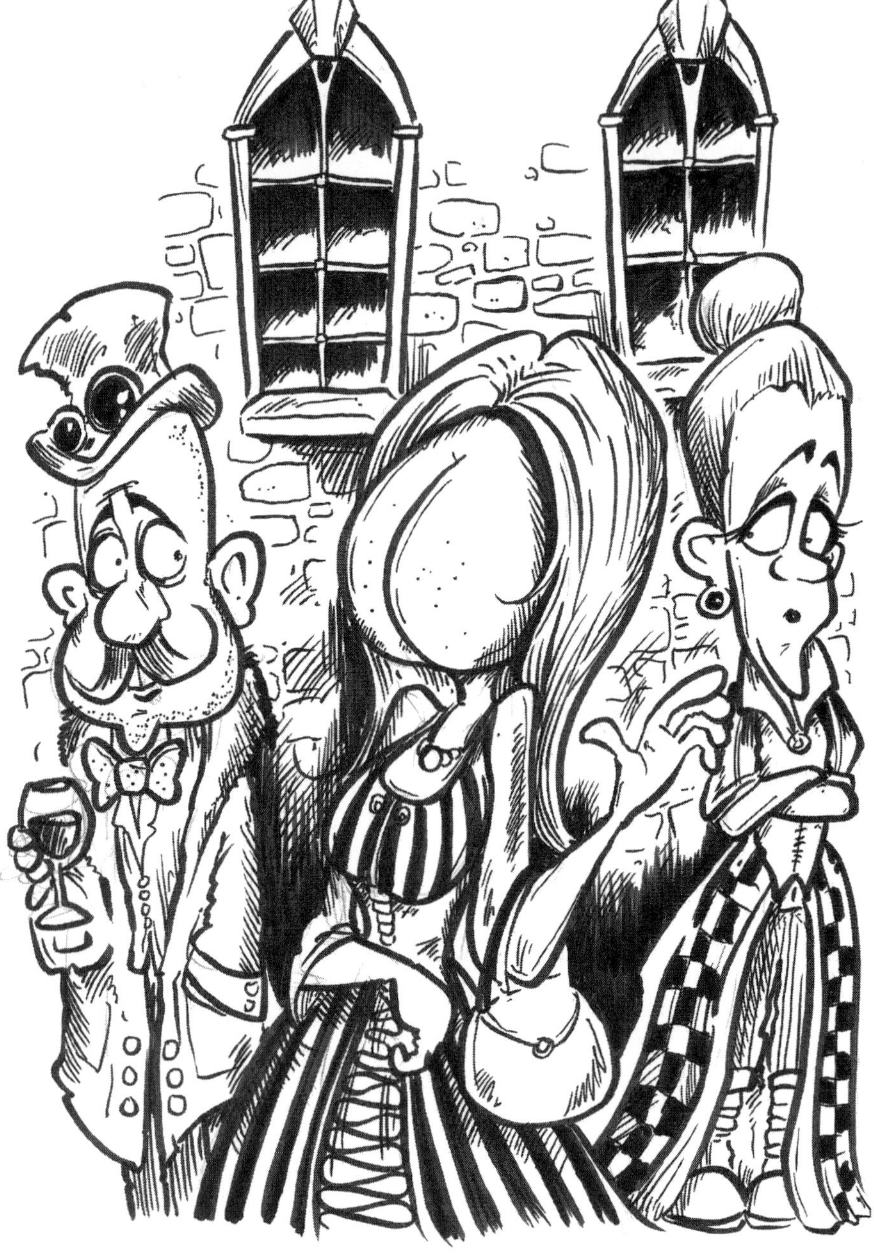

Straight away the press went nuts,
magazines paid high for celebs butts.
So the cameras just snapped away,
and her bum became the news next day.

Now her bum, it travelled round the nation,
as it was printed in every publication,
and soon Liz lost her fame and class,
as she soon became known as, "The Arse".

Desperate now to save her fame,
she played them at their own sick game,
and to get the press right off her case,
she wore a bum mask on her face.

She wore that mask everywhere she'd go,
at all events and at every show.
Thanks to her guts the press got bored,
and Liz became once more adored.

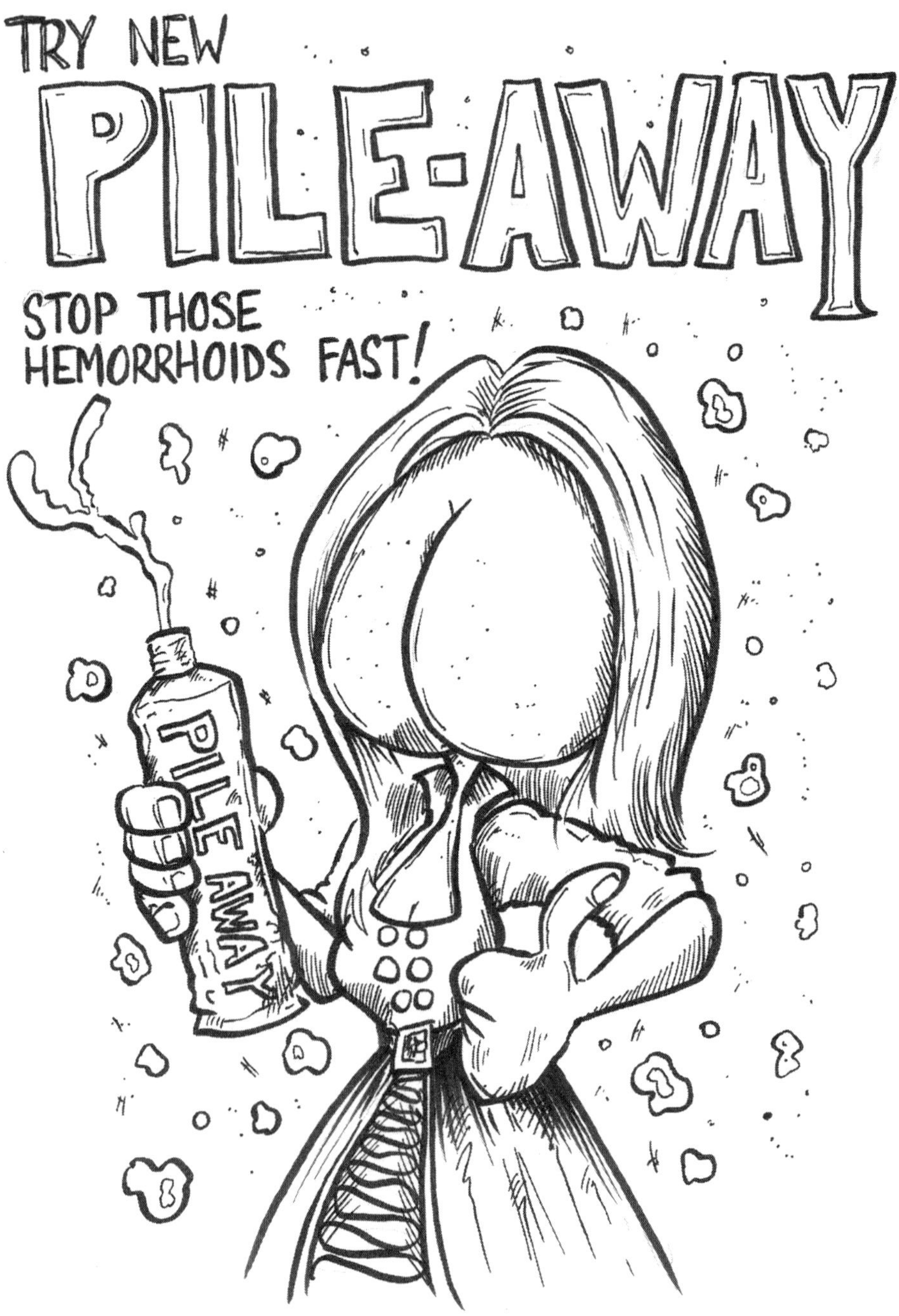
TRY NEW
PILE-AWAY
STOP THOSE HEMORRHOIDS FAST!
PILE AWAY

But Liz would now lose all her dreams,
for celebs you see use strange face creams,
and Lizzie's cream formed a kind of glue,
and the mask was stuck, no matter what she'd do.

Now folks would laugh and take the piss,
when Liz would talk or blow a kiss,
and her career had now gone so bad,
that her last job was a pile cream ad.

So now the joke's got kind of raw,
as Liz sips her food through a straw,
and now she's known in every place,
as the movie star with the arse-like face.

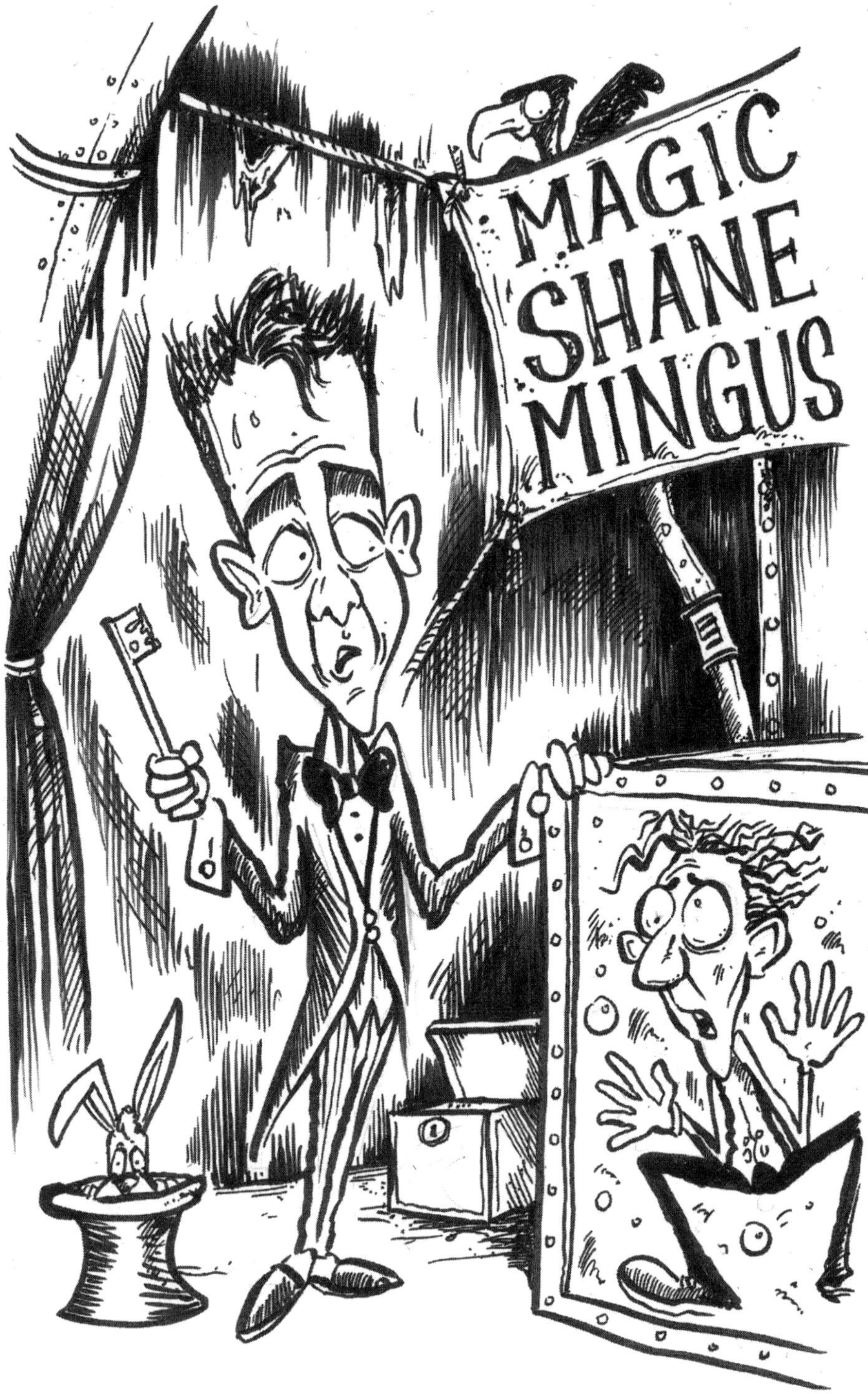
MAGIC
SHANE
MINGUS

**Shaky Shane Mingus
and his Magical Fingers**

In the city at night, a great place to go,
was to see Shane Mingus and his magical show.
Shane was an obsessive who got all his kicks,
by showing everyone his wild magic tricks.

Since he was a child he just loved to do magic,
but as time went on, it began to get tragic.
Soon Shane became shaky, as despite how he'd try,
on his final trick each night, his assistants would die!

His first assistant was a school friend called Tony,
who could cram into tight spaces as he was thin and bony.
They had a great trick, escaping a water filled box,
but alas, Tony drowned as Shane jammed up the locks!

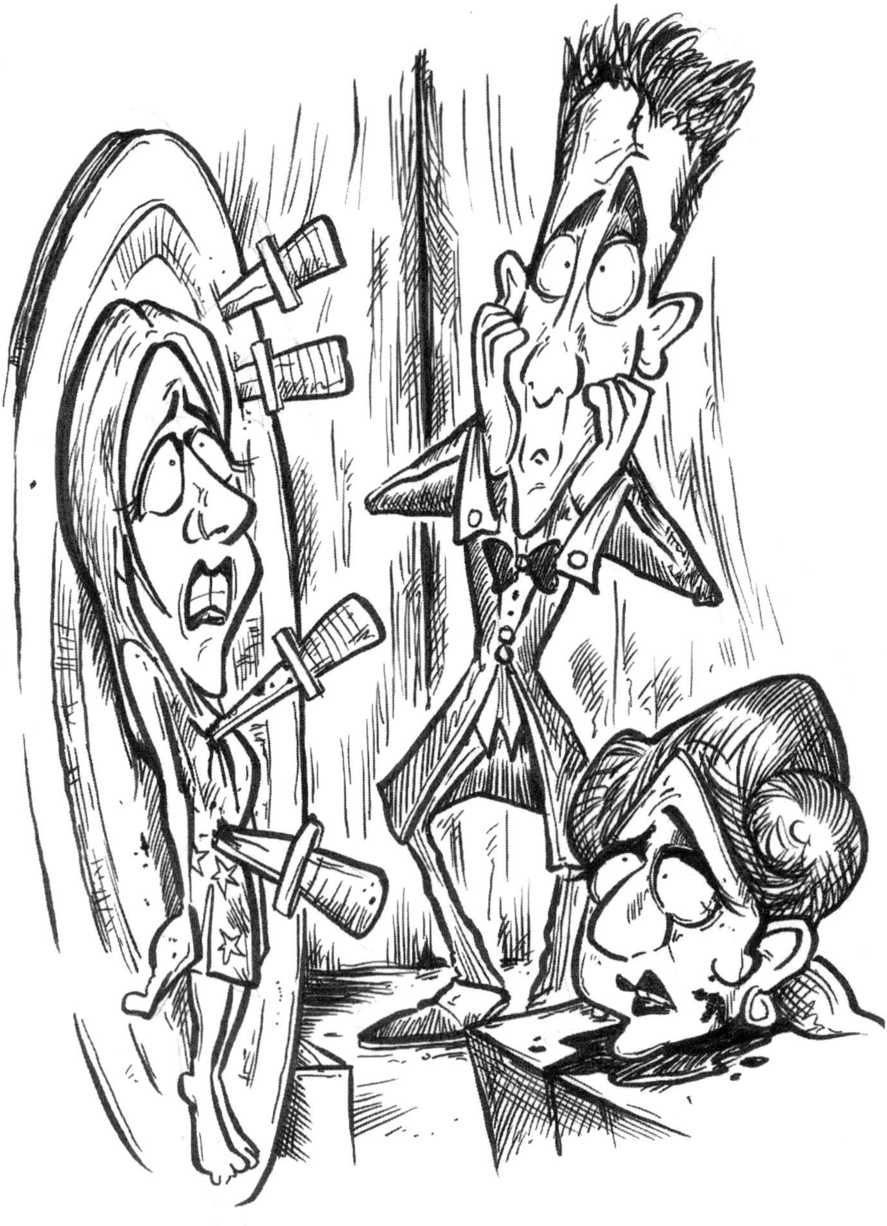

Next Shane used a girl just to stick to tradition,
and his sweet girl called Annie did great in audition.
But on her first night, in an amazing knife trick,
poor Annie was impaled, and the audience felt sick.

In the end getting desperate, he used a girl in the know,
a burlesque star called Chrissy who'd done this kind of show.
He thought he'd try an old favourite, a trick with a saw,
but he realised his mistake as her head hit the floor.

Soon, people wouldn't work with him on stage.
and poor nervous Shane struggled to earn a wage.
As his dangerous tricks had him so feared and hated,
he decided to run and so he emigrated.

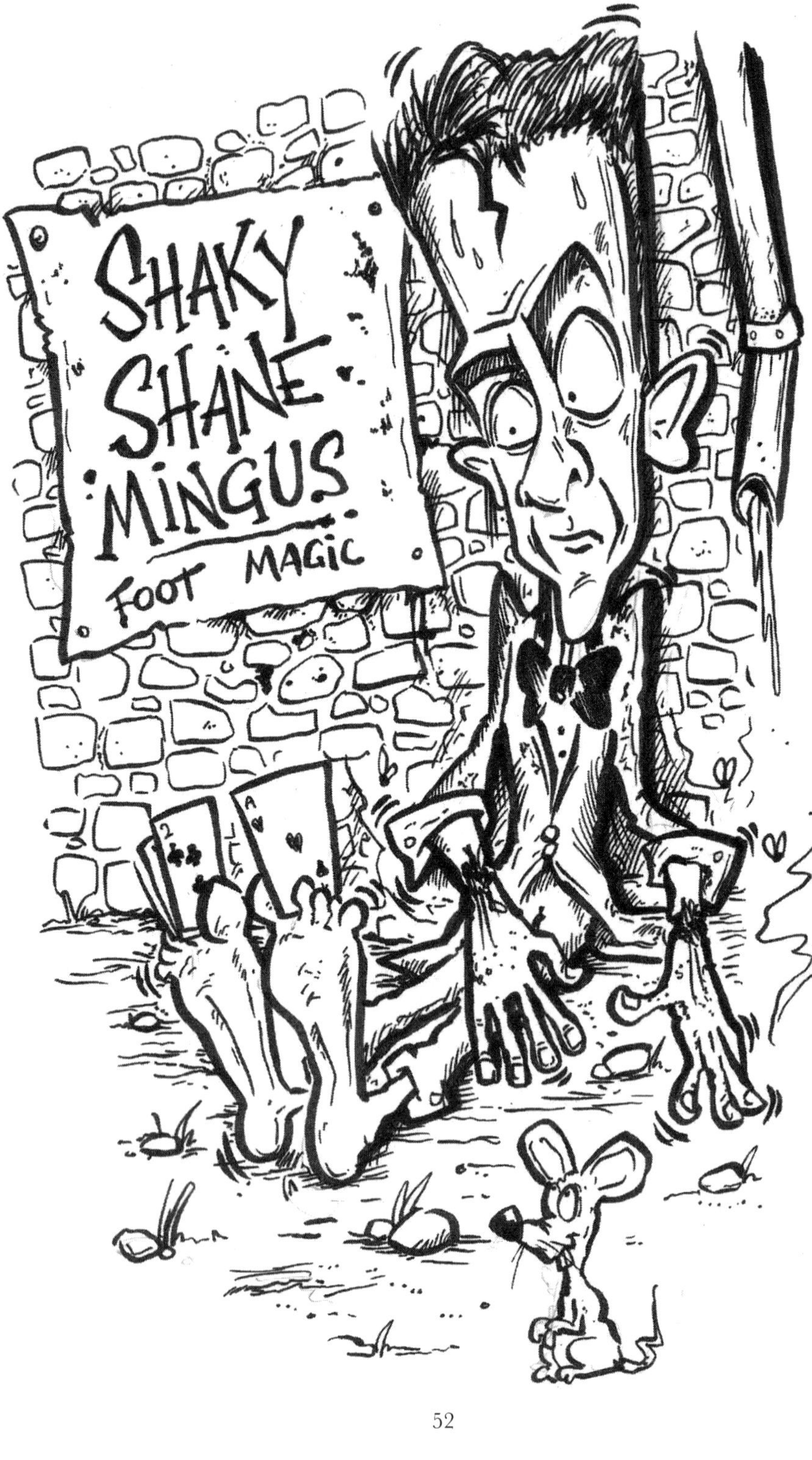
SHAKY SHANE MINGUS
FOOT MAGIC

Shane travelled far, to some strange distant lands,
and returned years later with a new pair of hands.
These new hands would hopefully make poor Shane rich,
for he'd been told these digits had belonged to a witch.

He'd bought the old hands at a travelling fair,
from a creepy old man with a sinister glare.
In a cheap surgery, blood sprayed all over the place,
as Shaky Shane Mingus had his old hands replaced.

So back in the city Shane had to wait a few days,
so that he could do tricks that would stun and amaze.
Once these old witch hands had regained their feeling,
they would surely show magic that would be so appealing.

But alas, now Shane has to do tricks with his feet,
for those hands on his wrists are just dead bits of meat,
and now his audience are always waiting for more,
for those tricks take him ages as he sits on the floor.

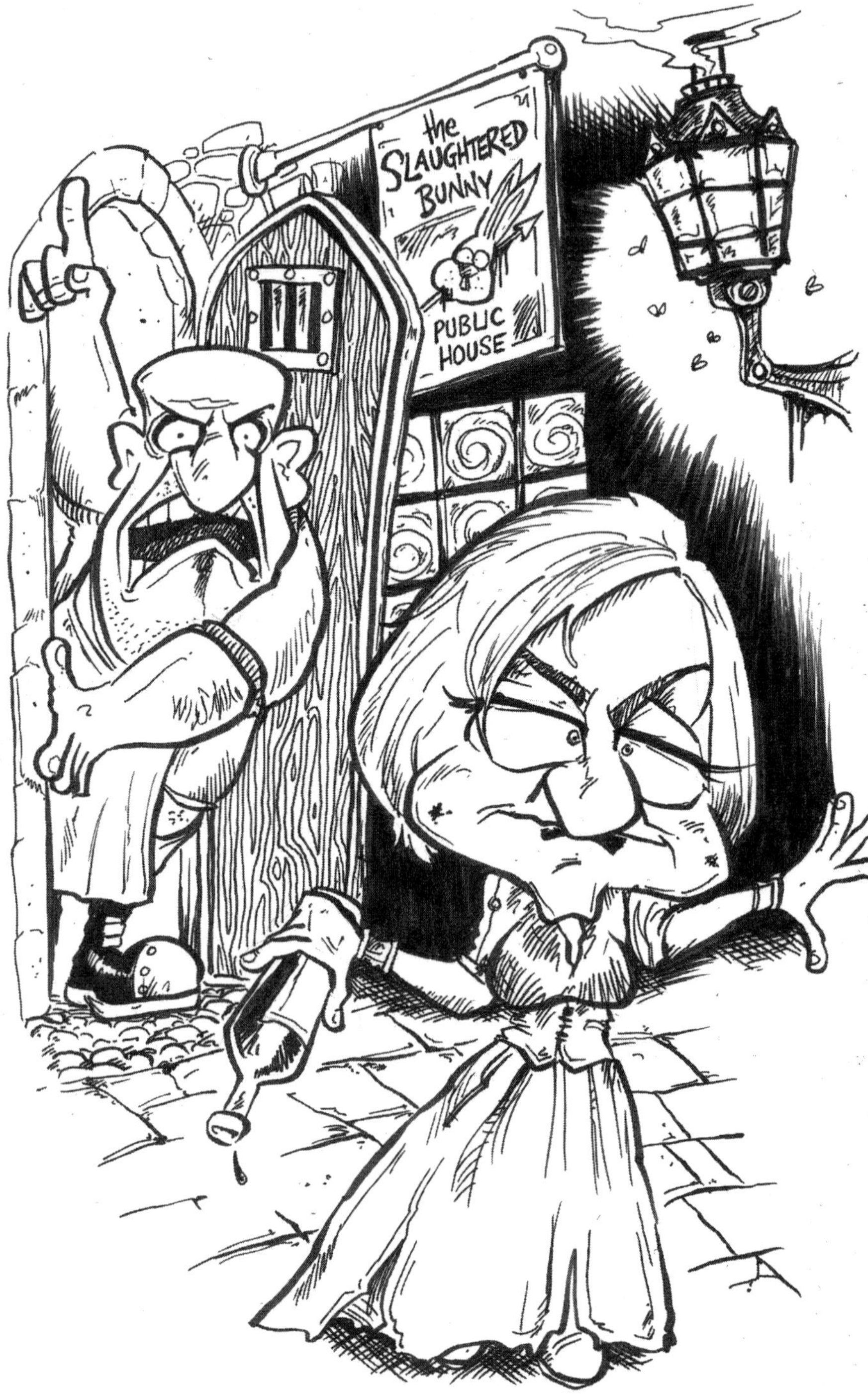
the SLAUGHTERED BUNNY
PUBLIC HOUSE

Laura La Gruff
the Girl Who Enjoys Bad Stuff

In the darkest alleys of Pity City,
lived a girl named Laura who's life weren't pretty,
She spent time in the worst drinking places,
surrounded by criminals and monstrous faces.

Living on Vodka, Whisky & Brandy,
she was eternally drunk and incredibly randy,
and so as not to become sober again,
she'd drink a bit more and chase all the men.

"You're barred from my pub!", the landlords would cry,
as she never paid, though she'd drunk them all dry.
.. and so slowly drunk Laura began to feel sober,
and screamed at one mother of a hangover.

Round and round the streets Laura raced,
desperate to become once more shit-faced.
But alas, no landlord had a warm enough heart,
to give free drinks to a mad drunken tart.

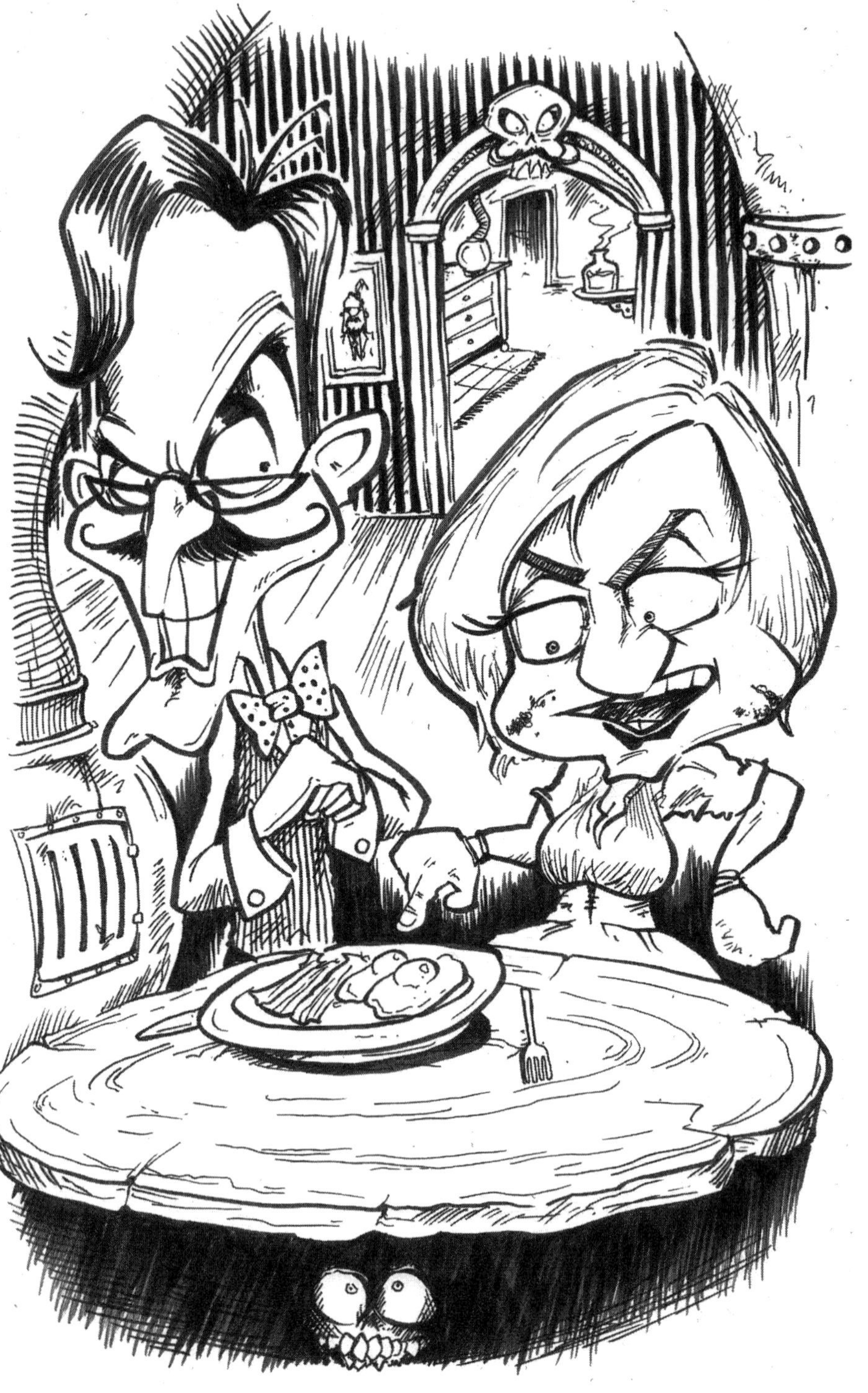

Sadly the strange alcoholic old nutter,
fell and collapsed in a manky old gutter.
As she lay there in dog's mess on the cold floor,
a kindly old gent stepped out from his door.

Feeling for the sad look on her face,
he promptly invited her into his place,
and slowly she entered on wobbly feet,
and he offered her comfort and something to eat.

"What's this!?" she cried, when he served up some lunch,
"you're lucky I don't just give you a punch!,
If I'd wanted to sleep with an old git who stinks,
he would first have had to supply me with drinks!"

Disaster would come from that violent outburst,
of all of her mistakes this one was the worst,
for this man was really an inventor of potions,
that could render you crazy and destroy emotions.

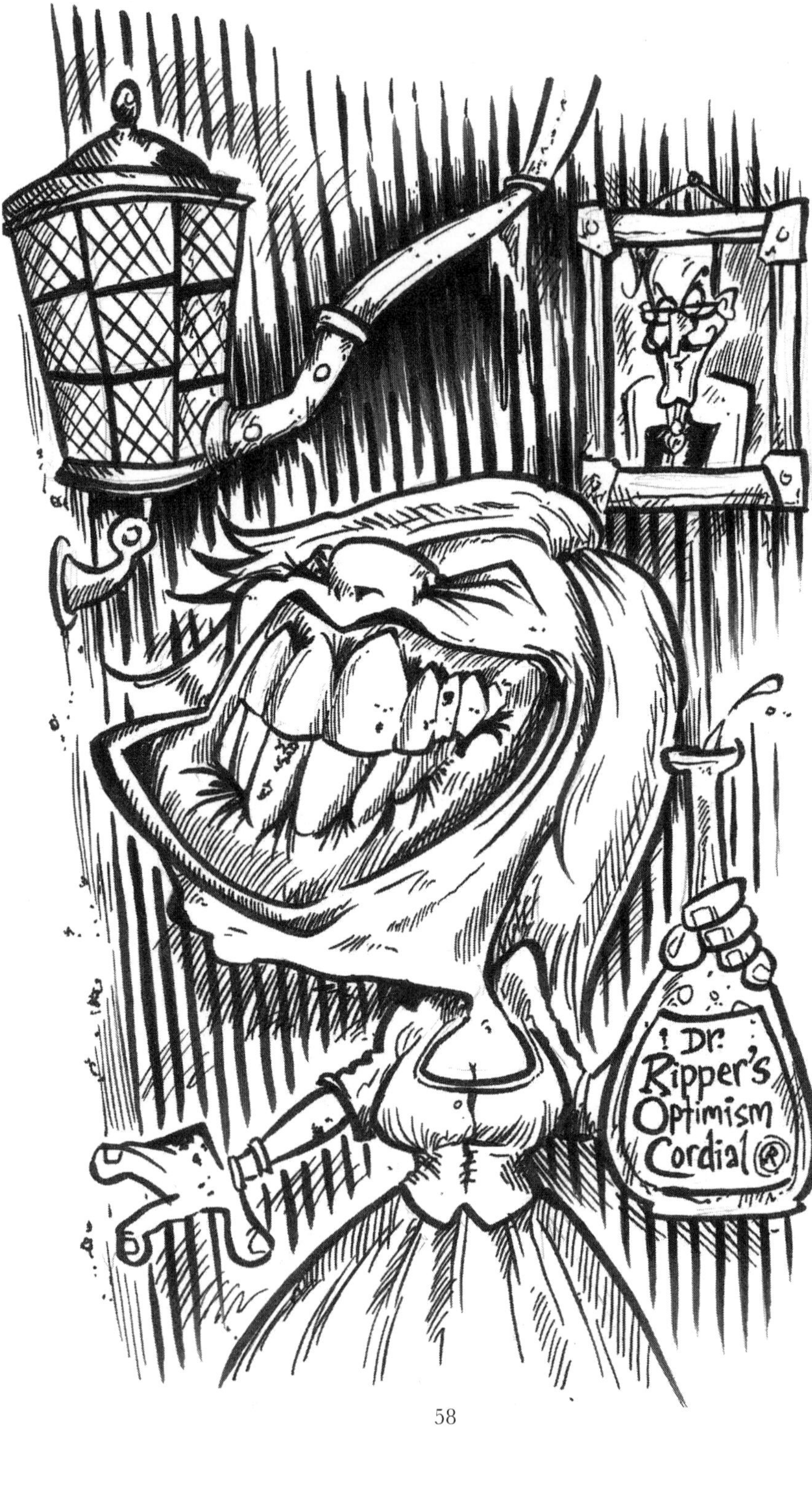
Dr. Ripper's Optimism Cordial

The old man just smiled and said, "I was mistaken,
I see you want drinks now, not my eggs and bacon."
So off the man went and returned rather quickly,
with a bubbling liquid that was all green and sickly.

So after she'd downed the "drink" he'd brought back,
she felt her brain pop, fizzle and crack.
Weird feelings coursed through her body like rockets,
and her bloodshot eyes span in their sockets.

Slowly her eyes ceased from their spinning,
her addiction to drink was now just the beginning.
For now Laura would always be happy,
to laugh and enjoy all things that were crappy.

For Laura is now truly insane,
though always smiling it causes her pain.
The worse things get the more that she laughs,
and her grin will now grow 'til her heads in two halves.

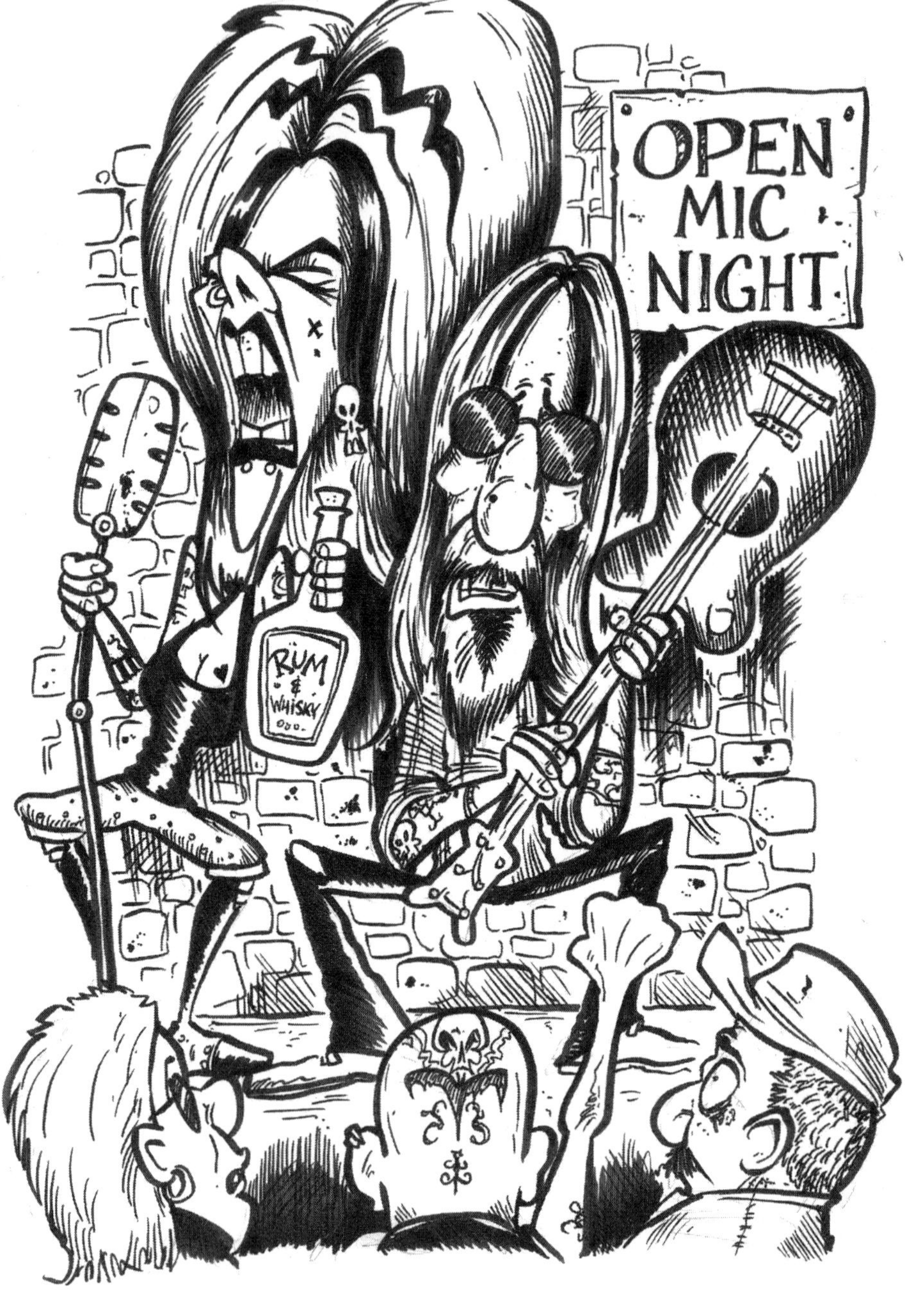
OPEN
MIC
NIGHT
RUM
&
WHISKY

Wild Dan Grand,
Who Ate His Own Band

In Pity City's darker alleys and streets,
on a Saturday night you'd hear wild beats.
From behind secret doors in the back of old pubs,
where you'd find the underground music clubs.

Crime bosses, drug dealers, ladies of the night,
They would all come here to get shit-faced and fight.
The bands would play all round the clock,
each trying to win in the War of Rock.

The war raged on, no-one would rest,
and it wasn't about who's band was the best.
For popularity in rock is rarely styled,
on who plays the best, but who's the most wild.

Some bands would smash up their guitars,
some bands would decide to smash up the bars.
Some singers would set fire to their own breath,
others would simply drink themselves to death.

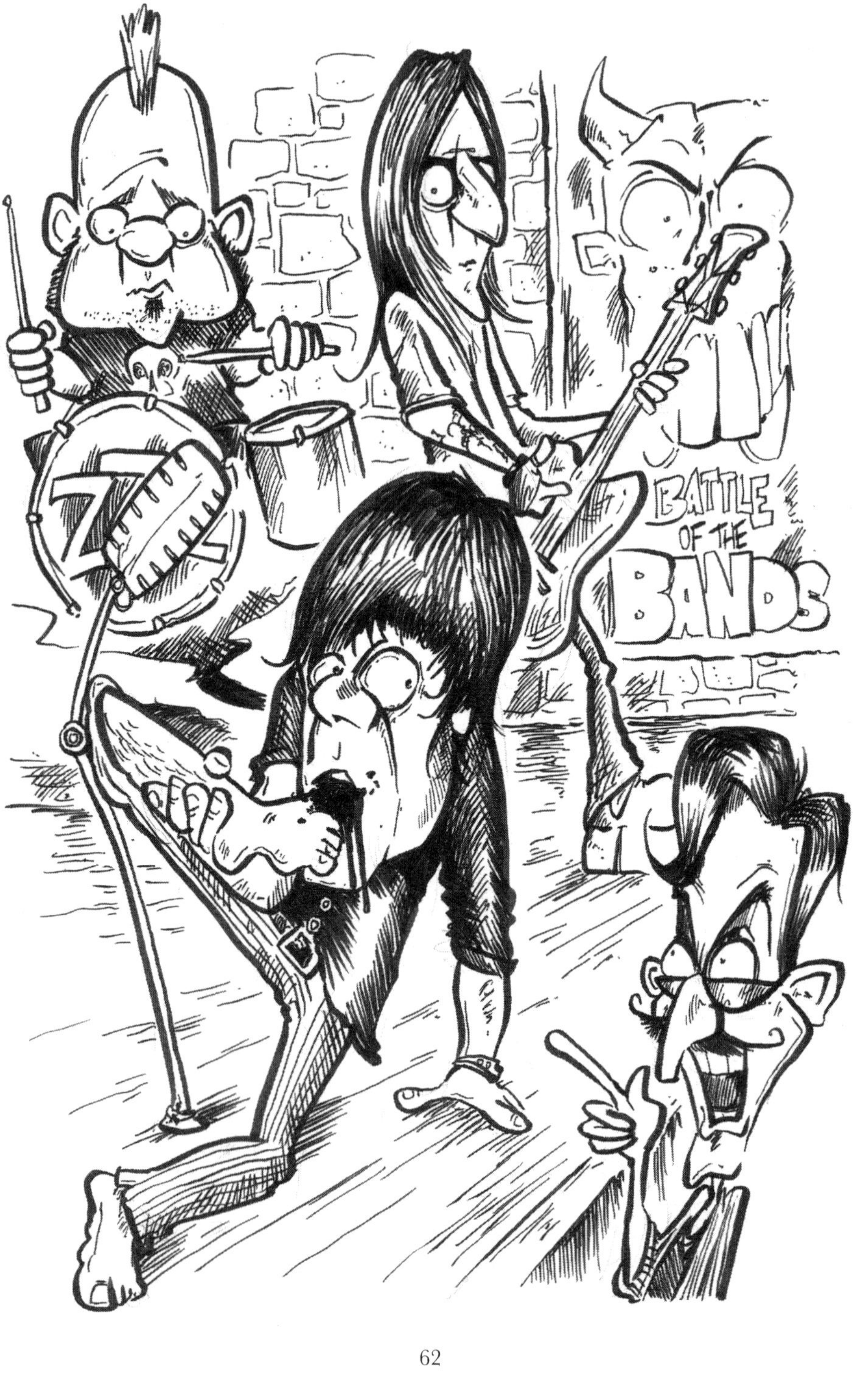
BATTLE OF THE BANDS

One band leader admired was Nikki Scarr,
who live on stage ate her own guitar,
.. and to the audience, as they were all wrecked,
it gained her an uncanny amount of respect.

Dan Grand, a singer who was not to be beaten,
realised respect came from shit that you'd eaten,
.. and Dan was certainly no coward,
as he searched for things that could be devoured.

He started off by eating his toe,
no music was playing but the crowd loved the show.
While that was digested he sang them a song,
and thought about eating more things that were wrong.

A voice from the crowd shouted to Dan,
"You think you're so tough, why not eat a man?!"
Dan suddenly realised the words from this geezer,
had summed up the answer, the final crowd pleaser.

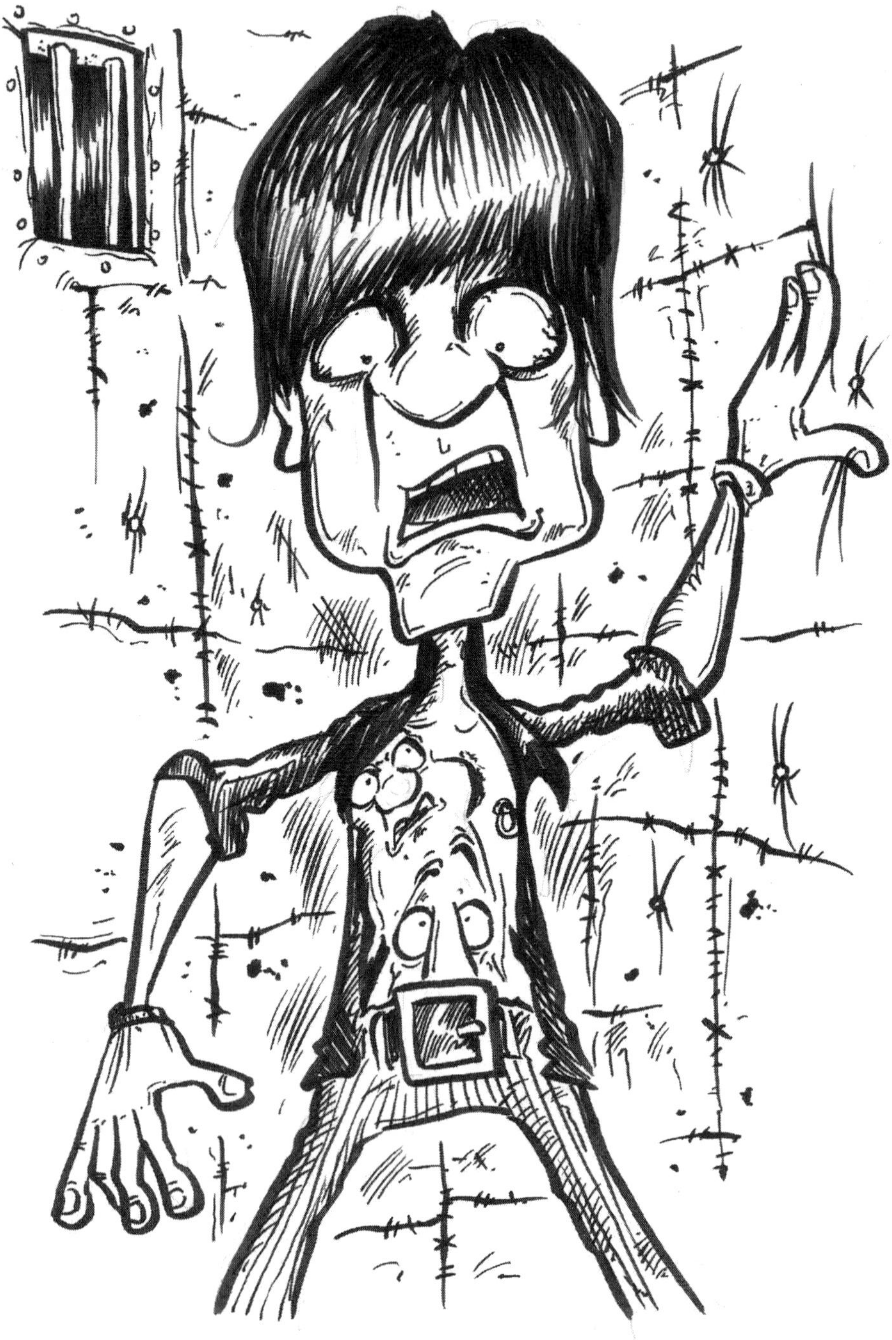

Suddenly Dan grabbed up his mic stand,
and started chasing around his whole band.
Within ten minutes his band were all dead,
and were slowly devoured between slices of bread.

While Dan sang and ate, the crowd looked on in shock,
this man had pushed too far the boundaries of rock,
..and by the time the band were ingested,
the crowds saw to it that he was arrested.

Sadly for Dan a strange reaction soon followed,
Thanks to drugs taken by those band mates he'd swallowed.
On Dan strange swellings appeared in odd places,
and those swellings looked just like Dan Grand's band mate's faces.

Now in his freak cell, Dan does his rock tour,
to a now much smaller audience of four.
For though by himself behind freak show gates,
he's convinced he's possessed by those other band mates.

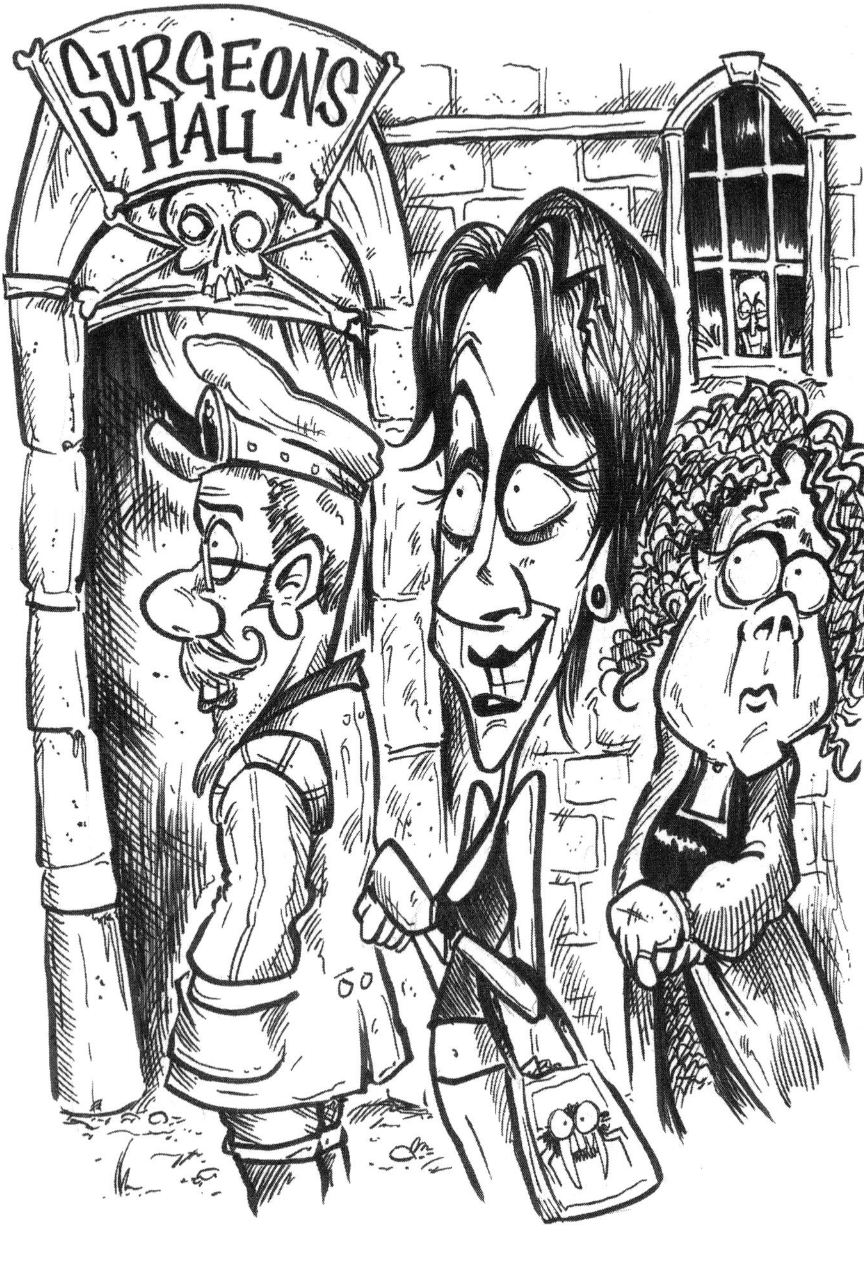
SURGEONS HALL

Scary Jade Sky
and the Self-Aware Eye

Mr & Mrs Sky were hippies by heart,
they simply loved nature, beauty and art.
But their daughter Jade didn't see what they saw,
she had a love of blood, violence and gore.

One day her sick nature received it's call,
when a show opened up at the new surgeon's hall,
.. and this gruesome show as I'm sure you would guess,
was full of body bits and much sticky mess.

"Oh yes!!", thought Jade as she stood in the queue,
"Imagine the gore and all the sticky goo!"
At 10am in walked all the curious,
but Jade quite quickly began to get furious.

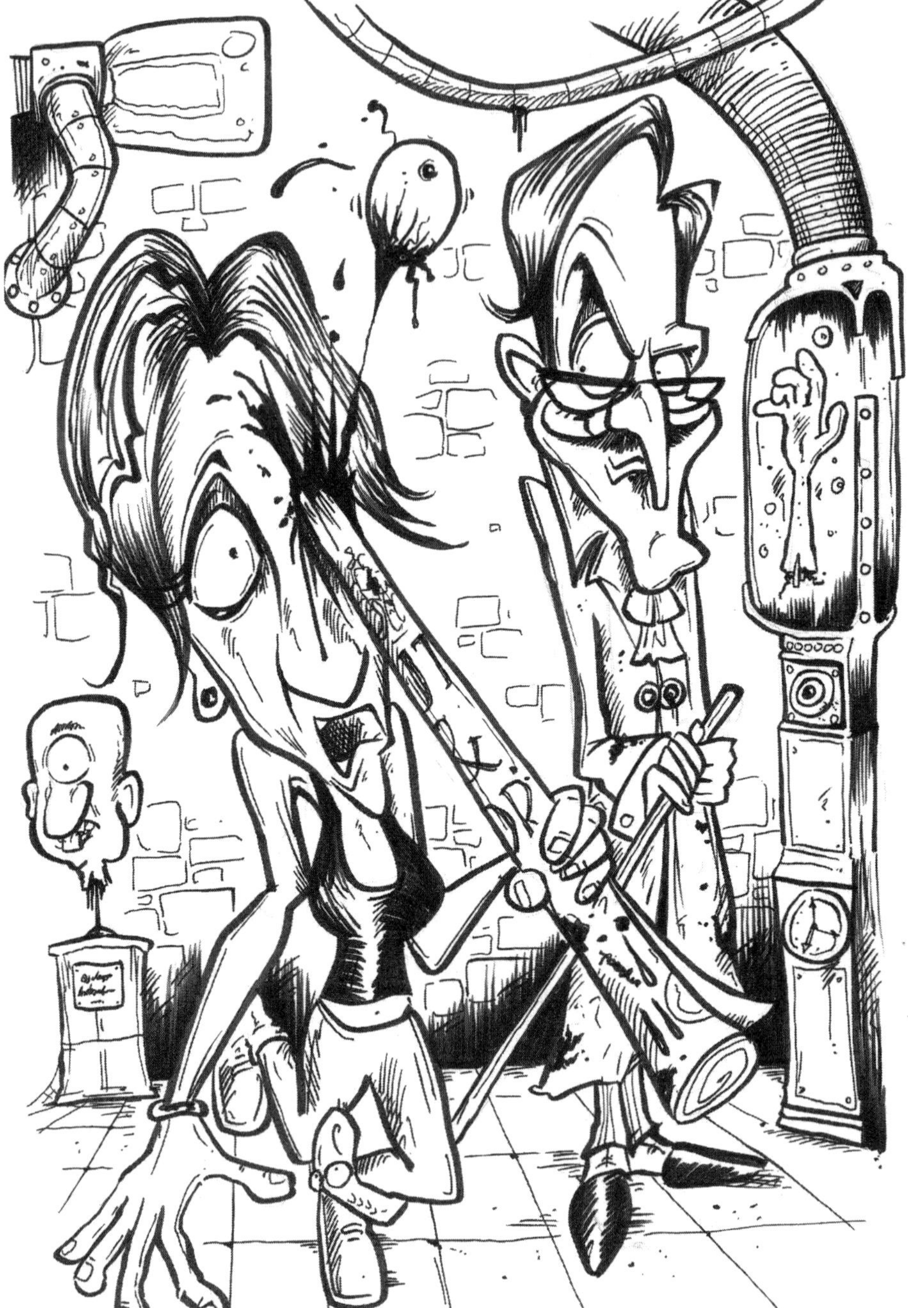

As although she'd explored, she'd had a good roam,
she realised she couldn't take any bits home.
She'd loved all the skulls and body parts she'd looked round,
but there was simply no gift shop anywhere to be found.

So it was as Jade started to depart the hall,
that she noticed a poster ensconced on the wall.
The poster was gory and really blood spattered,
and if missing surely it wouldn't have mattered.

So rolling it up, Jade departed quick,
but sadly she tripped on an old surgeon's stick.
The rolled poster flew up into Jade's eye socket,
and her eye popped out and flew off like a rocket.

TORTURE
VOMIT
COOKERY
MURDER FOR FUN
BLOOD
FRANKENSTEIN
SLIME

The surgeon grabbed Jade and despite her defiance,
he said he could help her with medical science,
and in a small room filled with blood, viens and bone,
the doc grabbed an eye that moved all on it's own.

He strode right over to where poor Jade sat,
and slammed that weird eye into her skull with a 'splat!'
Straight away Jade could see and felt in better health,
but that eye was still moving all by itself.

It may seem weird that Jade laughs and not cries,
as she sits there now with two different eyes,
but she's still a sick weirdo as she sits with that stare,
and there's not much more sick than an eye self-aware!

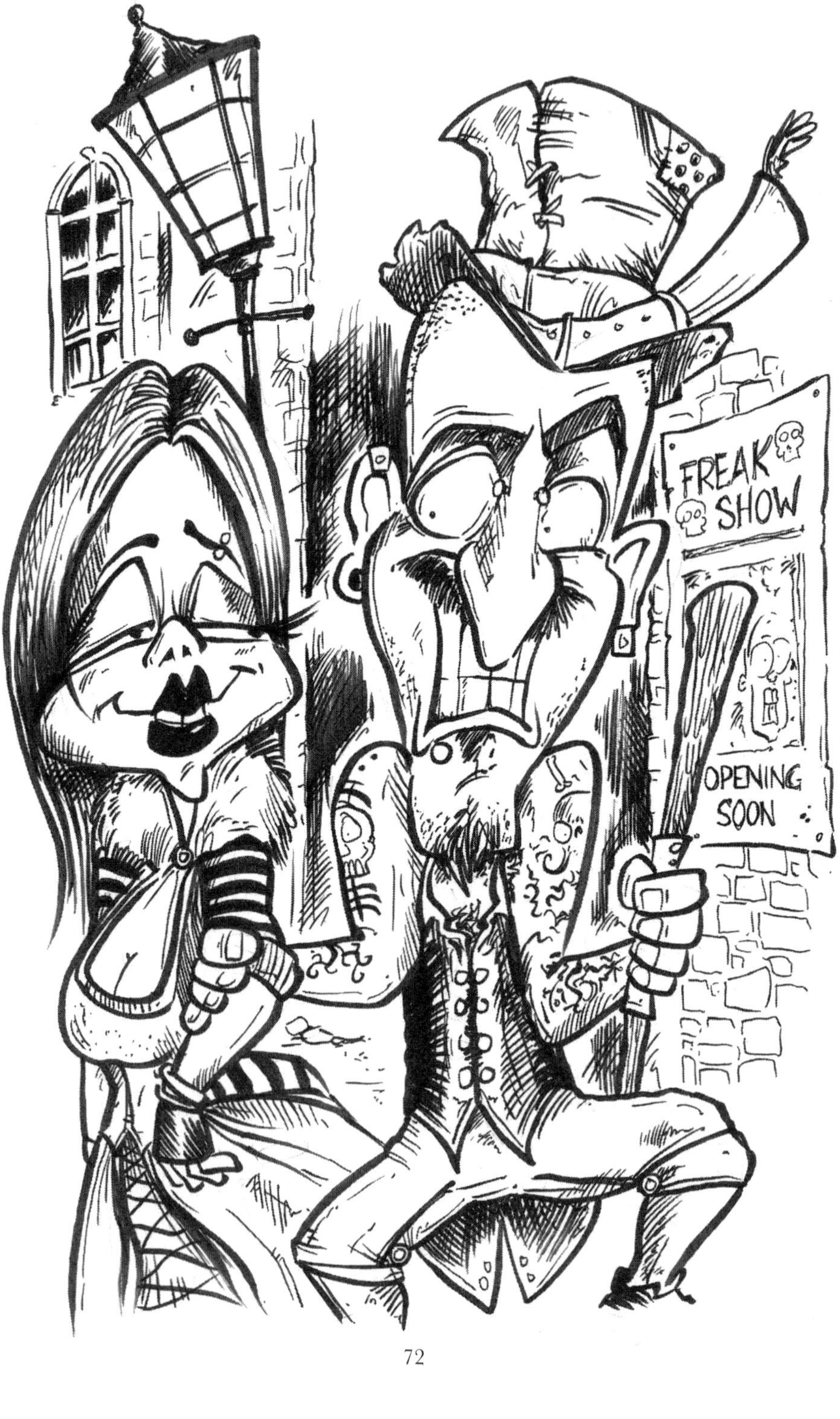
FREAK SHOW
OPENING SOON

The Sinister Tale of Dirty Joe Mace,
Who's Private Parts are in a Weird Place

It's not always the clean men, well groomed in smart fashions,
that to ladies alight those deep and dark passions.
Sometimes a good man just isn't enough,
and they fall for a good old fashioned bit of rough.

One such fellow was our own dirty Joe,
Who'd flash his shaved head and tattoos as he'd go,
parading up and down in the dark alleys,
hunting his next Dawn, Jane or Sally.

These unfortunate ladies would end up his prey,
and by morning Joe would simply just walk away.
The night would be over, he'd have done his dark deed,
no apology left, just his demon seed.

These events they did carry on for many years,
by night there was laughter, by morning was tears.
But soon there were no doubts, questions or maybes,
Joe was creator of many screaming babies.

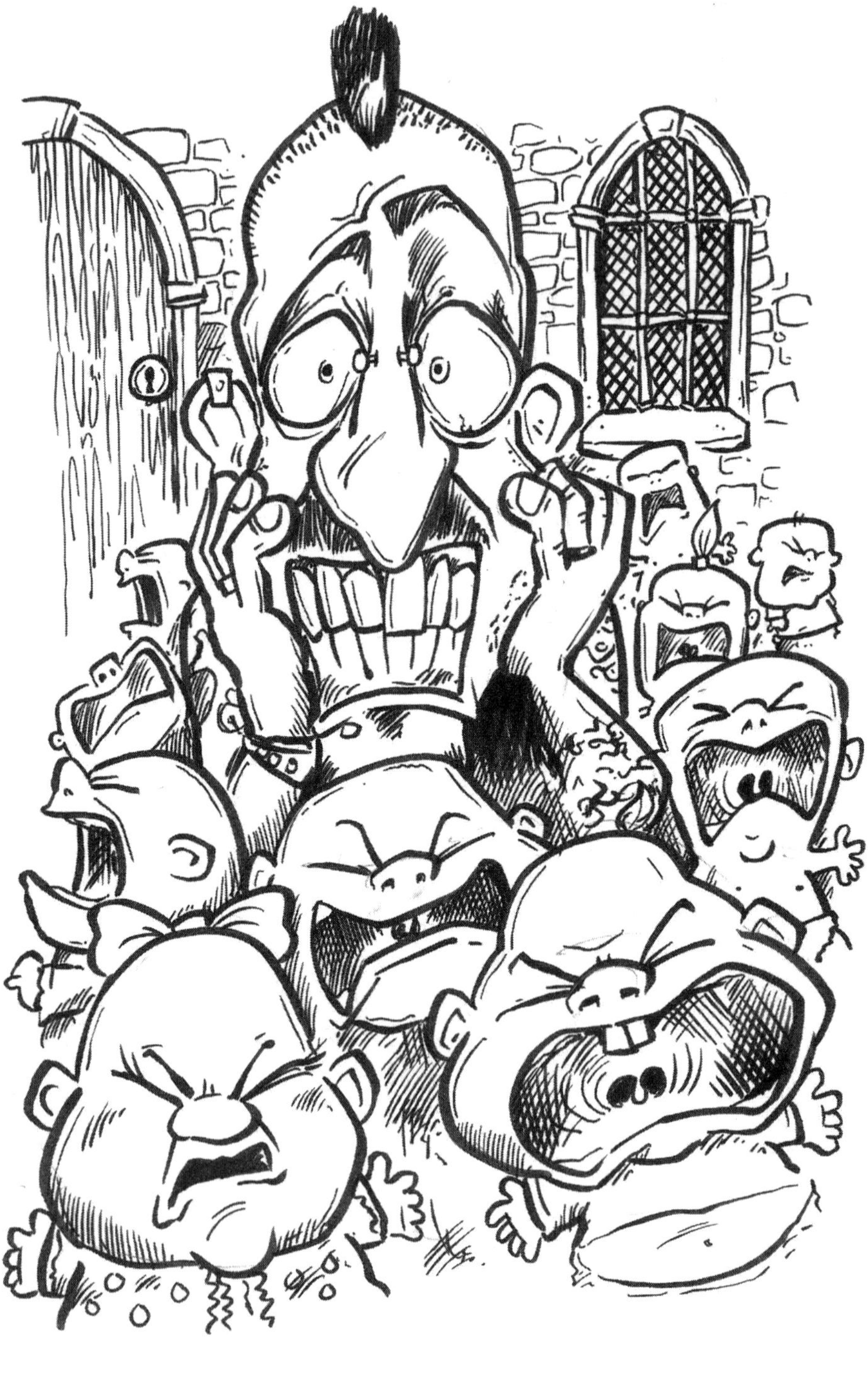

One day Joe was fated when a knock at his door,
revealed mothers a plenty who just wanted more.
Not more sex or more money or a wedding ring,
but babysitting duties for his screaming offspring.

While the ladies went off to their various jobs,
Joe was surrounded by these kids and their sobs.
He raced round the flat so very quick,
picking up toys and slipping in sick.

The screams just got louder, such an incredible din,
and Joe was so stressed he simply joined in.
Soon the mothers returned to Joe's elation,
for his nerves had been rocked to their foundations.

Though freed from his duties, Joe felt quite unwell,
and he rushed out the door, he must end this hell.
He ran to the clinic, they would do the job,
and he screamed to the staff, "Cut off my knob!"

CLINIC
PLEASE WAIT PATIENTLY PATIENTS!
KNOW THIS TOE?
ANAL WARTS
BEARD LICE
DEATH

The clinic didn't do that, that would have been silly,
it would have been extreme to just cut off his willy.
To just cut it off, would be dull I fear,
but to move it elsewhere... now there's an idea!

For if hard to reach, that thing would lose it's desire,
if in a weird place, it would put out it's fire.
So a surgeon stepped up, removed shaft, balls and sack,
and promptly relocated them onto his back.

So now on Joe's back, which is covered in ink,
there's a strange looking growth that makes passers-by think.
They stop and they stare, and then they take stock,
for among those tattoos, yes that's right, it's a cock!

But now out of sight, it has lost it's power,
and sex is a subject that to Joe is quite sour.
Now no longer able to use his pink sword,
Joe sits around feeling oh so very bored.

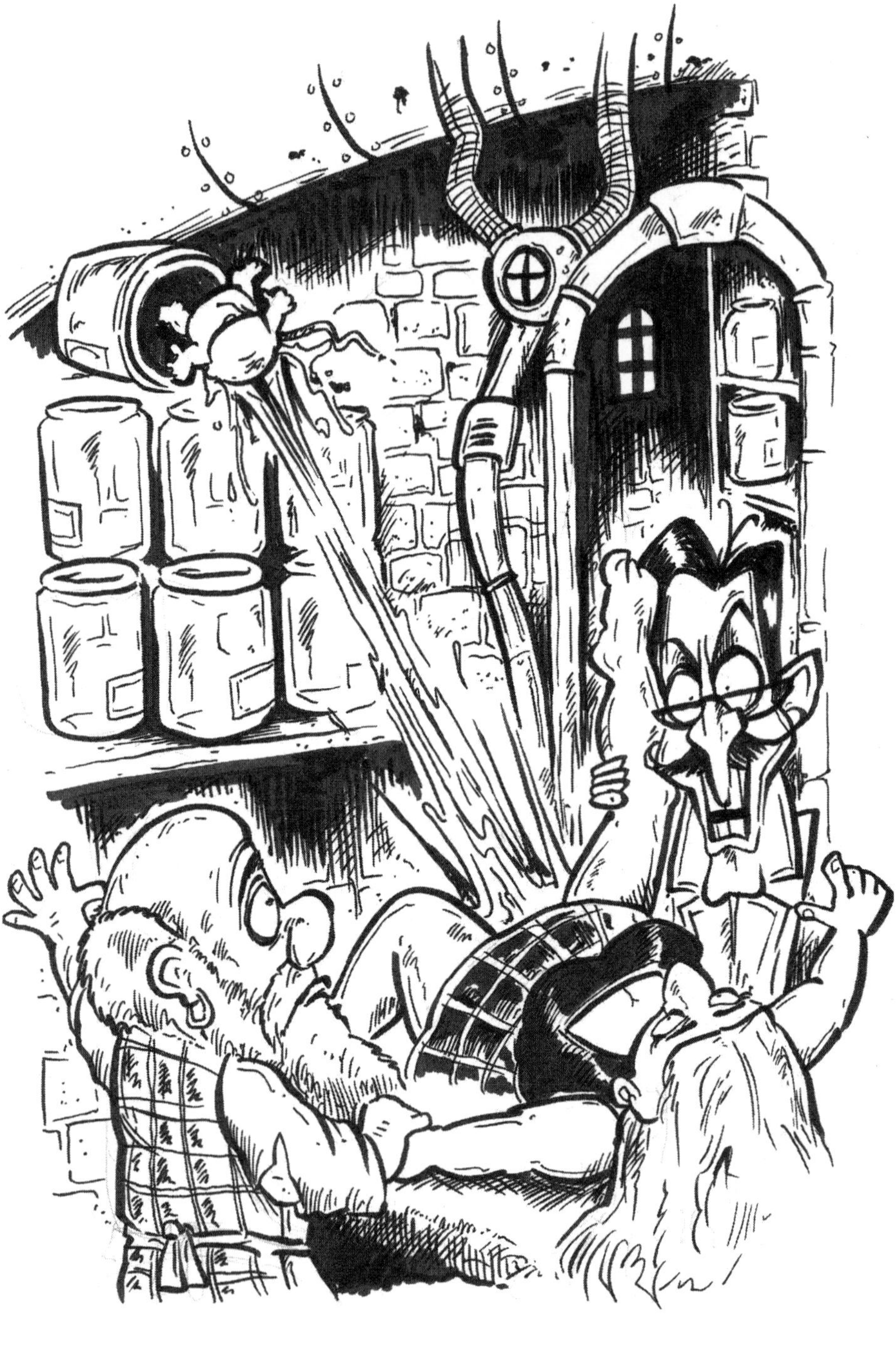

The Tale of Tiny Mary McDuff,
Very Small But Incredibly Tough

Far away in the highlands lived Arthur McDuff,
he lived with his wife and he invented stuff.
Of all of the things Arthur did make,
the most famous were jam jars that just wouldn't break.

These famous jam jars sold far and wide,
and they made McDuff rich and filled him with pride.
But his fortune faltered one dark stormy night,
when his wife gave birth by faint candlelight.

They had called for a doctor who had some strange ways,
because Mrs McDuff had been in labour for days.
The strange doctor gave her a curious potion,
and the baby shot out with a violent motion.

That baby had vacated it's mother's womb,
and disappeared somewhere into that dark room.
They searched in the darkness and fumbled around,
and inside a jam jar the baby was found.

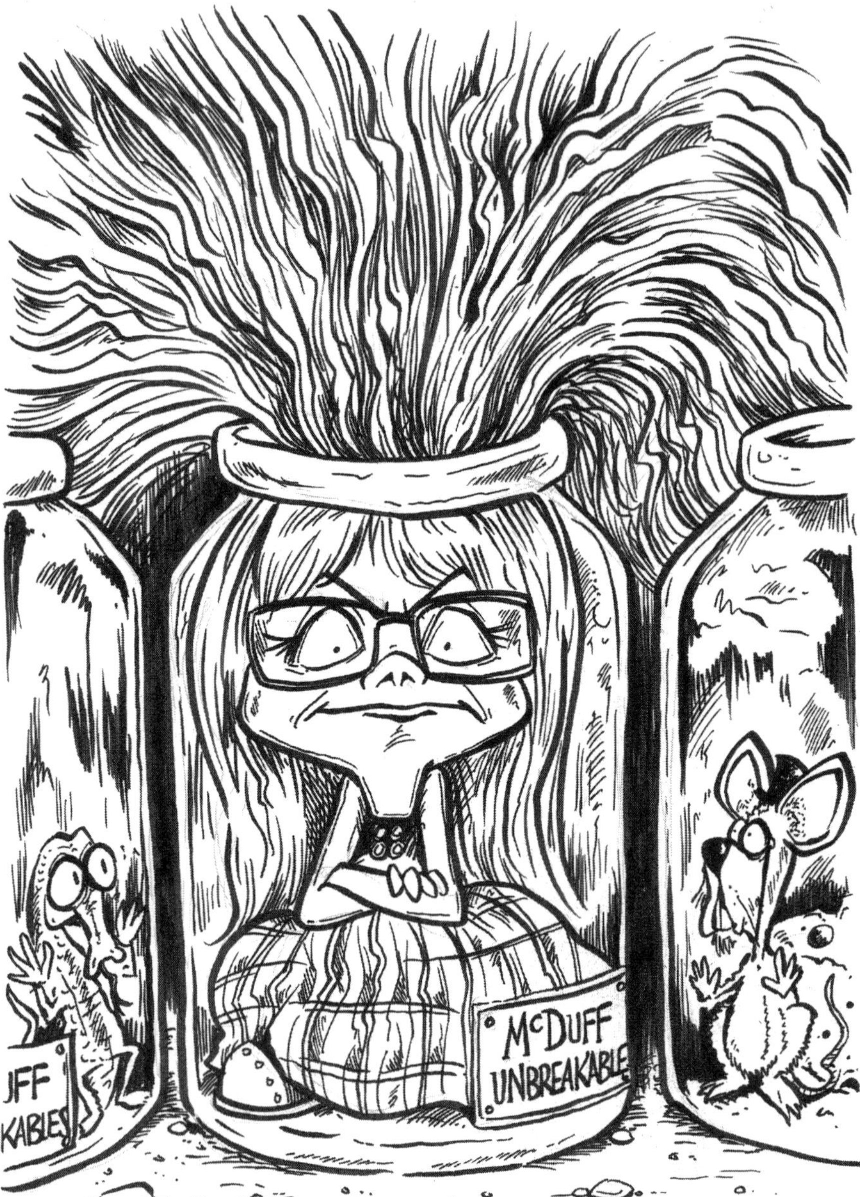
UFF
KABLES
McDUFF
UNBREAKABLE

The poor McDuffs were just so out of luck,
the jam jar was so strong the baby was stuck.
It soon became clear that as time would pass,
the child would grow up staring through glass.

They called the child Mary and she was so rare,
for though she remained tiny she grew fiery red hair,
that grew out of the jar all wild and free,
and she started to look like some strange sort of tree.

As she got to be older she started to stew,
her hair may be fiery but her temper was too!
She started to squeeze and she'd scream and she'd shout,
and one day the jar weakened and she smashed her way out!

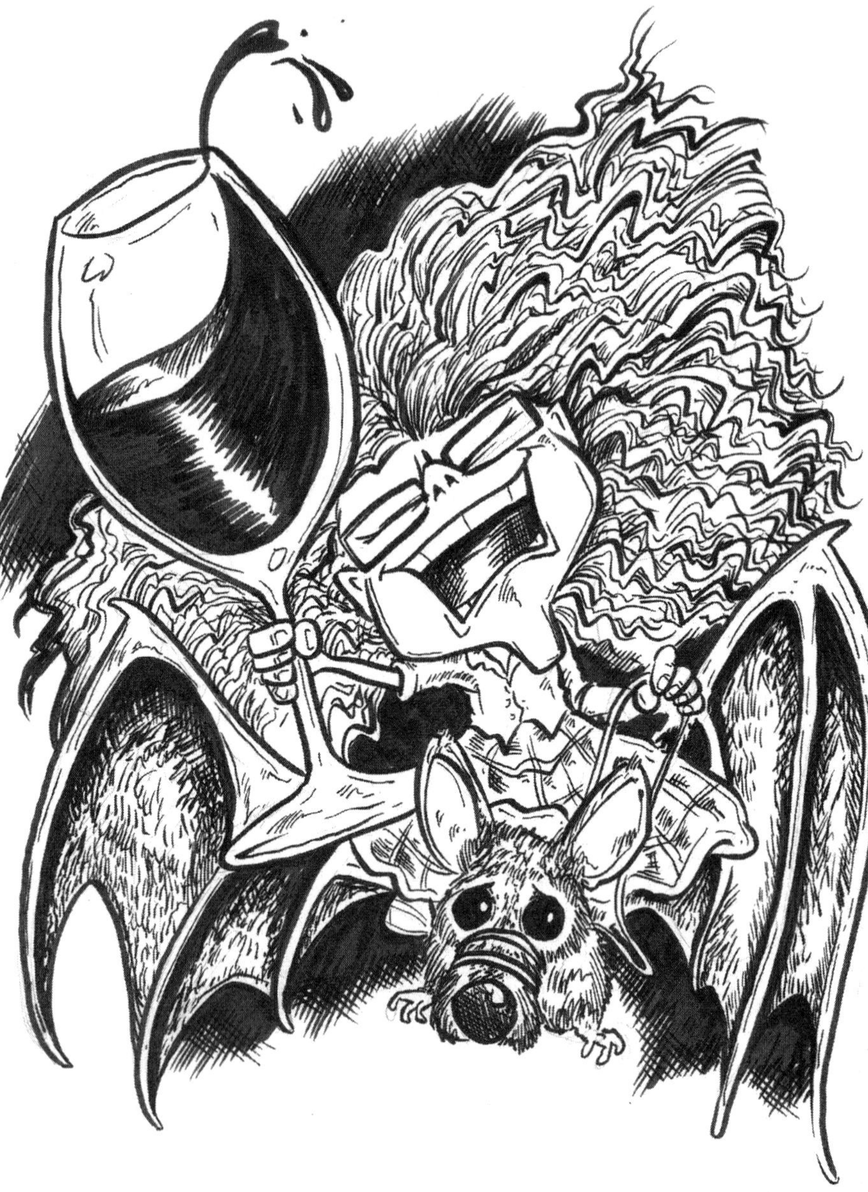

Tired of spending her life in one place,
Mary wanted to feel the wind on her face.
With a great big huge grin she ran round on the floor,
then she waved to her parents and shot out the door.

She travelled the world and saw all sorts of sights,
and she'd drink and be merry and get in some fights,
.. and so word got round that though Mary was small,
anyone that annoyed her would be some sort of fool.

So though Mary is laughing and always full of mirth,
heed my words and give her quite a wide berth.
For our little Mary does not suffer fools gladly,
just try it, annoy her, and she'll hurt you quite badly.

EXIT
Please visit the gift shop on your way out.
HAND SANITISER

And so we depart...

How did you find that? Everyone still breathing?
No headaches or nausea? No nosebleeds or heaving?
You may disagree but I will have no quarrel,
nothing you've seen here can be deemed immoral.

The creatures you've seen here were not born so fated,
their weirdness, their "freakishness" was all created.
This show was not intended for mocking the weak,
but rather to celebrate that they've reached their peak!

My freaks to whom I now close these gates,
were saved from the worst of all mankind's fates.
That fate so depressing, so grey and so formal,
NEVER be proud to be deemed as "normal"!

..and so I depart now and end these small ditties,
I'll be searching all of the villages, towns and cities,
collecting strange creatures as that's what I do,
be careful dear mortal, I might just collect YOU!

Author's note

While you may have noticed the mention of a whaling ship and an animal testing factory in the pages of this book, they are simply incidental to the storyline.
I by no means condone the behaviour of the sort of monsters that would harm animals and wish nothing but the worst of fates for such low-life individuals.

R. Nairn

About the author/illustrator

Rich Nairn is a cartoonist/caricaturist based in Kent, England who also goes by the name of
The Artful Doodler.

You can see many examples of his work by visiting his website at
www.theartfuldoodler.co.uk

For regular cartoon weirdness follow him on twitter: @richnairn
or watch his Youtube shows
"Tales from Doodle Manor"

Printed in Great Britain
by Amazon